Multicollinearity in linear economic models

# Tilburg Studies on Economics

# 7



A study on Econometrics

# Multicollinearity in linear economic models

D. Neeleman
*Professor of Statistics,
Free University of Amsterdam*

Foreword by
J.J.J. Dalmulder
*Professor of Econometrics and
Mathematical Economics,
Tilburg School of Economics,
Social Sciences and Law*

1973
Tilburg University Press
The Netherlands

Printed in Belgium

Distributors: Academic Book Services Holland, P.O. Box 66,
Groningen, the Netherlands

ISBN 90 237 2910 2

# Foreword

It was R. Frisch, who in his publications 'Correlation and Scatter Analysis in Statistical Variables' (1929) and 'Statistical Confluence Analysis by means of Complete Regression Systems' (1934) first pointed out the complications that arise if one applies regression analysis to variables among which several independent linear relations exist.

Should these relationships be exact, then there exist two closely related solutions for this problem, viz.

1. The estimation of 'stable' linear combinations of coefficients, the so-called estimable functions.
2. The dropping of the well-known condition of unbiasedness of the estimators.
   This leads to minimum variance minimum bias estimators.

This last solution is generalised in this book for the case of a model consisting of several equations.

In econometrics however, the relations among variables are nearly always approximately linear so that one cannot apply one of the solutions mentioned above, because in that case the matrices used in these methods are, although ill-conditioned, always of full rank.

Approximating these matrices by good-conditioned ones of the desired rank, it is possible to apply these estimation methods.

In order to get an insight in the consequences of this approximation a simulation study has been carried out for a two-equation model.

Two Stage Least Squares estimators and estimators found with the aid of the above mentioned estimation method have been compared.

The results of this study seem to be favourable for this new method.

More extensive research however is necessary to pass to a final sentence on the merits of this newly developed estimation method.

*J. J. J. Dalmulder*

# Contents

# I. Some remarks on linear economic models

## I.1 INTRODUCTION

The second paragraph of this chapter deals with linear economic models. Terminology and definitions in this paragraph are similar to those generally used.

The third paragraph deals with the identification problem as far as this is necessary to understand the following chapters.

Finally, the fourth paragraph, contains a short description of the 'multicollinearity' concept. A number of tests for finding and localising this phenomenon are described in a few words. The measures to be taken in the case of multicollinearity are dealt with in the following chapters.

## I.2 THE ECONOMIC MODEL

The construction of economic models has become increasingly important for the analysis of economic phenomena. Hence the attempt to give a description in this paragraph of what should be understood by an economic model.

*Definition 1.2.1*

An economic model is the mathematical representation of an economic 'theory'.

The term 'theory' is used in the sense given to it by Koopmans [1953] who defined it as follows: 'The combination of (a) principles of economic behaviour derived from general observation – partly through interview or experience – of the motives of economic decisions, (b) knowledge of legal and institutional rules restricting individual behaviour (tax schedules, price controls, reserve requirements, etc.), (c) technological knowledge, and (d) carefully constructed definitions of variables'.

Such a model usually consists of a number of equations showing the relations that are assumed to exist between more or less operationally defined variables. Generally speaking, economic relations have a *stochastic character* which means that they contain variables the properties of which are described with the aid of a distribution function. In this case one may speak of a *stochastic* model. However, it is often assumed by way of a simplification that variables may be observed as faultless and that the equations may be considered to be exact. In that case the model is called an *exact model.* Such a simplification is often useful as it facilitates the study of certain pre-statistical problems, e.g. the identification problem.

In this study we shall confine ourselves to linear economic models as (a) these models can be easily treated mathematically and (b) will certainly be satisfactory in practice as a first approximation to reality. In its most general form the stochastic linear model can be written as follows:

$$Az_t = \varepsilon_t \qquad (t = 1, 2, \dots, T) \qquad (1.2.2)$$

in which: $A$ represents an $m \times m$ matrix of coefficients ($m \leq n$) with rank $m$;

$z_t$ represents a column vector of $n$ variables observed as faultless at moment $t$;

$\varepsilon_t$ represents a column vector of $m$ non-observable error terms at moment $t$.

The error terms vector represents the joint effect of all these magnitudes, which are not stated in the equations system, as they, individually, would have a negligibly small influence on the relations.

The variables $z_{1t}, z_{2t}, \dots, z_{nt}$, the elements of vector $z_t$ may now be divided into (a) exogenous and (b) endogenous variables, which can be defined as follows:

*Definition 1.2.3*

An exogenous variable is a variable the value of which is, at any moment stochastically independent of the values of all the error terms at any moment.

*Definition 1.2.4*

A non-exogenous variable is called endogenous.

These definitions correspond with those of Koopmans and Hood [1953]. It should be noted that definition 1.2.3 implies that the values of the exogenous variables are determined within a system of equations which contains no endogenous variables, and which has not been inserted into the model. It is, therefore, sometimes said that exogenous variables are determined outside the model.

Another division of variables is a division into (a) predetermined and (b) dependent variables. These variables are defined as follows:

*Definition 1.2.5*

A variable is considered to be predetermined at moment $t$ when it is stochastically independent of all current and future error terms.

*Definition 1.2.6*

A variable which is not predetermined at moment $t$ is called a dependent variable.

These definitions, too, correspond with those of Koopmans and Hood [1953]. As to definition 1.2.5, it should be noted that this definition can be satisfied in two ways viz.:

1. exogenous variables satisfy this definition;
2. lagged endogenous variables satisfy this definition provided that for each moment $t$ the error terms vector $\varepsilon_t$ is stochastically independent of $\varepsilon_{t-1}, \varepsilon_{t-2}, \ldots$

If a model does not contain any lagged endogenous variables, the division into dependent/predetermined variables coincides with the endogenous/exogenous division. In what follows it has been assumed that this will always be the case.

With the aid of the definitions 1.2.5 and 1.2.6 above it will be possible, – after the variables have been re-arranged, if necessary – to split vector $z_t$ into a vector of dependent variables, hereafter to be denoted by $y_t$, and a vector of pre-determined variables, hereafter to be denoted by $x_t$.

Thus model 1.2.2 can be re-written as follows:

$$(B', C')\begin{pmatrix} y_t \\ x_t \end{pmatrix} = \varepsilon_t \qquad (t = 1, 2, \ldots T) \qquad (1.2.7)$$

or

$$B' y_t + C' x_t = \varepsilon_t \qquad (t = 1, 2, \ldots T) \qquad (1.2.8)$$

in which: $B'$ represents an $m \times s$ matrix of coefficients;

$C'$ represents an $m \times (n\text{-}s)$ matrix of coefficients;

$y_t$ represents the column vector of the $s$ dependent variables at moment $t$;

$x_t$ represents the column vector of the $n$-$s$ predetermined variables at moment $t$;

$\varepsilon_t$ represents the column vector of the error terms at moment $t$.

*Definition 1.2.9*

A model is called a complete model when $B$ represents a square matrix with rank $m$.

This means that, when the values of the error terms and the predetermined variables at moment $t$ have been given, the dependent variables can be determined at moment $t$.

If in future the term 'model' is used a complete model is meant unless explicitly stated otherwise.

*Definition 1.2.10*

Model (1.2.2) when written as follows:

$$y_t = \pi' x_t + \eta_t \qquad (t = 1, 2, \ldots T) \qquad (1.2.11)$$

in which:

$$\pi' = -(B')^{-1} C'$$

$$\eta_t = (B')^{-1} \varepsilon_t$$

is called the reduced form of the model.

This means that dependent variables are written as linear combinations of predetermined variables and error terms. Forms (1.2.7) and (1.2.8) of the model may – in order to be distinguished from the reduced form – also be called: the structural form of the model.

The same distinction is made with regard to the parameters. The elements of matrix $\pi'$ are called the reduced form parameters of the model, and the elements of the matrices $B'$ and $C'$ the structural form parameters of the model.

If the model consists of one equation only, the reduced and structural forms coincide.

## I.3 THE IDENTIFICATION PROBLEM

Before dealing with the description of the identification problem it will first be necessary to introduce the 'structure' concept.

*Definition 1.3.1*

A model in which all structural parameters have been given a numerical value and in which the distribution function of the error terms has been completely specified, is called a structure.

Consequently a model may be considered to be a set of structures. It may however very well be possible that this set contains more elements that are not contrary to the observations made and to the 'a priori' conditions if available, not even if the number of observations is extended indefinitely. In such a case we speak of a non-identifiable model. As to the identification problem, we now have to deal with the question under what conditions it would be possible to determine – totally or partly – the structure on the basis of the observations made and the 'a priori' conditions.

From the above formulation of the identification problem it readily appears that this is a fundamental problem which plays a part in many sciences.

It is therefore not a typically econometric problem and is certainly not restricted to the model described in the preceding paragraph.

The fundamental characteristics of the general identification problem can be found in Koopmans and Reiersøl [1950].

In econometrics there are two special cases which have been thoroughly analysed. Particularly the so-called 'one equation error on variables model' by Neyman [1937] and Reiersøl [1950] and the 'linear simultaneous equations model' described in the preceding paragraph. The latter model was discussed by Koopmans and Rubin [1950] for the case of linear restrictions on coefficients, whilst generalisations for non-linear models and non-linear restrictions were given by Wald [1950] and Fisher [1959, 1961, 1963].

A more general discussion of the identification problem was recently published by Rothenberg [1969].

Part of the 'linear simultaneous equation model' theory will be discussed below, for the sake of completeness and as far as this is necessary for the following chapters.

This means that only the case of homogeneous linear restrictions on

coefficients matrix $A$ will be considered. The following is applicable to this particular case only. First of all we shall assume that the error terms meet the following three requirements:
1. the expectation of $\varepsilon_t$ equals zero for each value of $t$;
2. the covariance matrix of $\varepsilon_t$ represented by $\Sigma$ is independent of $t$;
3. $\varepsilon_t$ and $\varepsilon_\theta$ are stochastically independent for $t \neq \theta$.

It is the first property which enables us to convert the stochastic model

$$Az_t = \varepsilon_t \tag{1.3.2}$$

into an exact model as follows:

due to the fact that the number of observations can be extended indefinitely it will be possible to determine the distribution of the endogenous variables, if the exogenous variables have been given, and, consequently, we may write:

$$E(y_t|x_t) = \pi' x_t \tag{1.3.3}$$

Determination of the conditional expectation (1.2.3) yields:

$$B' E(y_t|x_t) + C' x_t = 0 \tag{1.3.4}$$

being a form which corresponds with the exact model, on the understanding that the observations $y_t$ have been replaced by the corresponding conditional expectations $E(y_t|x_t)$.

Consequently we can confine ourselves to discussing the problems of the exact model, in which case it will be necessary to formulate the identification problem as follows:

under what conditions will it be possible to determine the coefficients matrix uniquely when it is assumed that the number of observations may be increased indefinitely.

Now this problem may be replaced by another and simpler problem, viz.:

under what conditions will it be possible to determine a certain row of matrix $A$ uniquely, when it is assumed that the number of observations may be increased indefinitely.

It stands to reason that once the conditions, under which a certain equation of the model can be identified, have been found, it will be possible to examine all equations of the model, one by one, with the aid of these conditions. If all rows of $A$ can be determined then the model has been identified.

By way of example, let us assume that we wish to ascertain if the first equation of the model has been identified and let us assume that this row of $A$ is denoted by $a'_1$.

Unless we have further information it will not be possible to identify $a_1$. For it stands to reason that when the observation vectors $z_1$ up to and including $z_T$ are combined to form matrix $Z$, $Z$ must hold:

$$a'_1 Z = 0 \tag{1.3.5}$$

but also

$$AZ = 0 \tag{1.3.6}$$

so that not only $a'_1$ but all row vectors of $A$ are to be found in the row kernel of matrix $Z$. But this means that without further information a linear combination of row vectors of $A$ cannot be distinguished from $a_1$.

The 'a priori' information needed to arrive at an identification can take various forms. In this study we will confine ourselves to 'a priori' information in the form of homogeneous linear restrictions on $A$ coefficients.

Which means restrictions of the form:

$$a_{11}\phi_{11} + a_{12}\phi_{21} + \dots + a_{1n}\phi_{n1} = 0 \tag{1.3.7}$$

in which $\phi_{11}$ up to and including $\phi_{n1}$ are known numbers, whilst at least one of these numbers does not equal zero.

These restrictions can be written in the form:

$$a'_1 \phi_1 = 0 \tag{1.3.8}$$

in which $\phi_1$ is a column vector of the numbers $\phi_{11}$ up to and including $\phi_{n1}$. Thus the restrictions e.g. for the first equation of the model may be summarized as:

$$a'_1 \Phi = 0 \tag{1.3.9}$$

in which $\Phi$ is an $n \times r$ matrix when $r$ restrictions are made for $a'_1$-coefficients.

The restrictions made for $a'_1$ by 'a priori' information and the restrictions resulting from the observations can be summed up as follows:

$$a'_1 (Z, \Phi) = 0 \tag{1.3.10}$$

If there is a vector $a_1$ satisfying the restrictions of (1.3.10) then vector $ca'_1$, in which $c$ represents an arbitrary constant, will also satisfy these restrictions. It will then be possible to determine vector $a'_1$ fully with the exception of the scale factor. This leads to the following definition:

*Definition 1.3.11*

An equation is called identifiable under 'a priori' conditions if and only if the coefficients of this equation with the exception of a scale factor can be determined.

From (1.3.10) the following theorem readily appears:

*Theorem 1.3.12*

A necessary and sufficient condition for identification of the first equation is, that $R(Z, \Phi) = (n-1)$, in which $R(Z, \Phi)$ represents the rank of the matrix $(Z, \Phi)$.

*Proof*

1. Assume $a'_1$ to be identifiable and $R(Z, \Phi) < (n-1)$ then there will be a vector $v \neq ce_1$ with $e'_1 = (1, 0, 0, \ldots, 0)$ so that $v' \, A(Z, \Phi) = 0$; but then $a'_1$ is not identifiable which contradicts the assumption.
2. Assume that $R(Z, \Phi) = (n-1)$ and $a'_1$ is not identifiable, which means there is a vector $v \neq ce_1$ with $e'_1 = (1, 0, 0, \ldots, 0)$ so that $v' \, A(Z, \Phi) = 0$; but then $R(Z, \Phi) < (n-1)$ which contradicts the assumption.

From this theorem it readily appears that a necessary condition for identification of the first equation is that $\Phi$ has at least $(m-1)$ columns. For it is obvious that $R(Z, \Phi)$ should equal $(n-1)$ and that $R(Z) = n - m$. The latter follows from (1.3.6) and from the requirement that the model should be complete.

This condition is known as the order condition.

*Order condition*

A necessary condition for identification of the first equation is that the number of 'a priori' restrictions on the coefficients of this equation is larger than or equal to $(m-1)$.

The following theorem shows a form, which is easier to handle, as to the necessary and sufficient condition for identification of theorem 1.3.12 since this theorem does not contain the matrix of observations $Z$.

This form is known as the rank condition for identification.

*Theorem 1.3.13*

A necessary and sufficient condition for $R(Z, \Phi) = (n-1)$ is that $R(A\Phi) = (m-1)$.

*Proof*

1. As $R(A)=m$ and $R(\Phi)\geq(m-1)$: $R(A\Phi)\leq m$. As moreover $a_1'\Phi=0$, it follows that $R(A\Phi)\leq(m-1)$. Assume that $R(A\Phi)<(m-1)$ then there is a vector $v\neq ce_1$ so that $v'\,A\Phi=0$ which means that $v'\,A(Z,\Phi)=0$ whilst $v'\,A\neq ca_1'$ but then $R(Z,\Phi)<(n-1)$ which contradicts the assumption.
2. Assume that $R(Z,\Phi)<(n-1)$ then there is a vector $v'\,A\neq ca_1'$ so that $v'\,A(Z,\Phi)=0$ which means that $v'\,A\Phi=0$ in which $v\neq ce_1$, but then $R(A\Phi)<(m-1)$ and this contradicts the assumption.

From this theorem follows:

*Rank condition*

A necessary and sufficient condition for identification of the first equation is that $R(A\Phi)=(m-1)$.

A case which often occurs in practice is that the 'a priori' information only consists of zero restrictions.

These are conditions in which each $\phi_i$-vector of $\Phi$ contains only one figure one and for the rest only zeros. Thus one specifies in fact that certain $A$-coefficients equal zero. If the variables are arranged in such a way that the last $m^{xx}$ endogenous variables and the last $k^{xx}$ exogenous ones of the first equation carry a coefficient zero, it readily appears from theorem 1.3.13:

*Theorem 1.3.14*

A necessary and sufficient condition for $R(A\Phi)=(m-1)$ is that $R(\pi'_{1\cdot 2})=(m^x-1)$, in which $m^x=m-m^{xx}$ and $\pi'_{1\cdot 2}$ is the matrix consisting of elements which belong to the first m$^x$ rows as well as to the last $k^{xx}$ columns of $\pi'$.

*Proof*

Premultiplying $A\Phi$ by $(B')^{-1}$ one finds

$$(I,\ -\pi')\ \Phi=\Phi_1-\pi'\Phi_2$$

in which:

$\Phi_1$ represents the matrix consisting of the $m$ first rows of $\Phi$;

$\Phi_2$ represents the matrix consisting of the $(n-m)$ last rows of $\Phi$ whilst

$\Phi_1-\pi'\Phi_2$ is a matrix of the form:

$$\begin{pmatrix} 0 & -\pi'_{1\cdot 2} \\ I_{m^{xx}} & -\pi'_{2\cdot 2} \end{pmatrix}$$

in which:

$I_{m^{xx}}$ represents the unit matrix of $m^{xx} x m^{xx}$;

$\pi'_{2\cdot 2}$ represents the matrix consisting of elements which belong to the last $m^{xx}$ rows as well as to the last $k^{xx}$ columns of $\pi'$.

The theorem can now easily be drawn up.

In view of the following chapters it is of importance to discuss the difference in under-identified, completely identified and over-identified equations.

*Definition 1.3.15*

An equation is called completely identified if the rank condition has been satisfied and if the number of columns of $\Phi$ equals $(m-1)$.

*Definition 1.3.16*

An equation is called over-identified if the rank-condition has been satisfied, and if the number of columns of $\Phi$ is larger than $(m-1)$.

This means that there will be two or more different (but not necessarily disjunct) sets of 'a priori' restrictions so that the equation will become exact-identified with the aid of either set.

*Definition 1.3.17*

An equation is called under-identified or non-identifiable when neither definition 1.3.15 nor definition 1.3.16 is satisfied.

It should be observed that, if two or more variables are linear-dependent, the theorems derived above will no longer be valid. If this linear dependence concerns the variables appearing in the equation to be identified, the equation is non-identifiable. When this is not so then it will be not possible to make a statement without further investigation. We shall revert to this later on.

## I.4 MULTICOLLINEARITY

*Definition 1.4.1*

If, within a set of variables, one or more linear relations exist it is said that these variables are multicollinear.

The reason why multicollinearity is of such an importance is that, if it is present, there is a possibility that the equation in question is under-identified and consequently cannot be estimated. Once multicollinearity has been detected several solutions are available for this problem. The detection of multicollinearity raises various difficulties. It will, in practice, seldom occur, however, that there is an exactly linear relation between the various variables.

However, as is often the case in economics, various variables will be strongly correlated.

Farrar and Glauber [1967] treated in an article a number of tests on multicollinearity which are very easy to apply. Tests have been designed for:

a. Detecting multicollinearity;
b. Localising the multicollinearity;
c. Finding the multicollinearity pattern.

The authors' starting-point is that $z_t$ follows a normal $n$-dimensional distribution and they then define multicollinearity as a significant derivation of orthogonality. The tests are explained below.

*ad a. Detection of multicollinearity*

Assume that

$$Z = \begin{bmatrix} z'_1 \\ \vdots \\ z'_T \end{bmatrix} \qquad (1.4.2)$$

is a matrix of $T$ observations of the $n$-dimensional stochastic variables $z_t$.

Without losing generality it can be said that the $z_t$-elements have been standardized. In that case $|Z'Z|$ will be the determinant of the $z_t$ correlation matrix. It is known that this determinant becomes zero when there is complete dependency and becomes one when the variables are orthogonal.

In other words:

$$0 \leq |Z'Z| \leq 1 \qquad (1.4.3)$$

The following test statistic is based on this property.

$$\chi^2_{|Z'Z|}(v) = -[T-1-1/6(2n+5)] \ln |Z'Z| \qquad (1.4.4)$$

On the condition that the variables are mutually independent, it can be shown that this statistic has the $\chi^2$ distribution with $v = 1/2n(n-1)$ degrees of freedom.

This last has been proven by Bartlett [1950], who used a result obtained by Wilks [1932].

*ad b. Localisation of multicollinearity*

If the test described above has shown that multicollinearity exists, the second step will be the localisation of multicollinearity.

The test statistic designed for this is:

$$W = (z^{ii} - 1)\left(\frac{T-n}{n-1}\right) \tag{1.4.5}$$

in which:

$z^{ii}$ is the $i^o$ diagonal-element of the inverse correlation matrix $(Z'Z)$.

On the condition that $z_i$ is independent of the variables $z_1, \ldots, z_{i-1}, z_{i+1}, z_{i+1}, \ldots, z_n$ it can be shown that this statistic has an $F$ distribution with $(n-1)$ and $(T-n)$ degrees of freedom. Here again use is made of Wilks' results [1932].

This test should be applied for each variable in order to trace the multicollinear sub-set.

*ad c. The multicollinearity pattern*

Having found the multicollinear sub-set it often seems useful to study the pattern of the mutual relations in this sub-set.

The following test is used for this purpose:

$$t_{ij} = \frac{z_{ij}\sqrt{T-n}}{\sqrt{1-z_{ij}^2}} \tag{1.4.6}$$

in which:

$$z_{ij} = \frac{-z^{ij}}{\sqrt{z^{ii}}\sqrt{z^{jj}}} \tag{1.4.7}$$

$z^{ij}$ is the $(i, j)$ element of the inverse of the correlation matrix $(Z'\,Z)$.

Provided $z_i$ and $z_j$ are mutually independent the test statistic has the $t$ distribution with $(T-n)$ degrees of freedom.

This test should be applied to each pair of $z_i$ and $z_j$ in the multicollinear sub-set.

It has been shown that measures have to be taken, in the case of multicollinearity. If 'a priori' information is available either in the form of equalities or inequalities between coefficients or of a subjective probability distribution of coefficients, various solutions are offered by a number of authors.

We should like to mention Drèze [1962, 1968], Theil [1963], Theil and Goldberger [1961] and Zellner [1961].

If 'a priori' information is not available attempts should be made to estimate 'stable' linear combinations of coefficients, the so-called estimable functions.

If one does not like to be restricted in this way, there is also the possibility of using the so-called best linear $P$-unbiased estimation method.

The following chapters will treat the theory of this in detail. However, exact multicollinearity has been taken as starting-point. In practice this form of multicollinearity hardly occurs so that, before the theory is applied, matrix $Z$ should be approximated by means of an exactly multicollinear matrix having the rank found with the aid of, e.g., the test developed by Lawley [1956]. Chapter IV will deal with this subject.

# II. Best linear $P$-unbiased estimators for a one-equation model

## II.1 INTRODUCTION

In this chapter the best linear $P$-unbiased estimators for a model consisting of one equation and any given covariance matrix will be derived.

In the second paragraph we shall discuss the three classical hypotheses underlying the model.

The third paragraph contains a derivation of the best linear unbiased estimators of the classical model. These estimators are the well-known (generalised) least-squares estimators, the theory of which already occurs in the works of Gauss [1809] and Markof [1900]. In the course of years writers extended and generalised this theory. We should mention here Aitken [1935], Neyman and David [1938], Parzen [1961] and Rao [1945[a], 1945[b], 1946]. If the model is extended so that the classical hypotheses of absence of multicollinearity and non-singularity of the covariance matrix are left out of account, it is impossible to determine best linear unbiased estimators of the coefficients of the equation. There are two, closely related, solutions to this problem. The first solution is to restrict oneself to the determination of best linear unbiased estimators of so-called 'estimable functions' i.e. linear functions of the coefficients of the equation. This theory has been developed particularly by Rao [1962, 1965, 1966], Mitra and Rao [1968] and Khatri [1968]. The theory can be found in paragraph four.

The second solution of the above-mentioned problem, described in paragraph five, is found by generalising the concept of 'unbiasedness'. If this concept is generalised as indicated by Penrose [1956], it is possible to determine best linear $P$-unbiased estimators. This theory has been developed e.g. by Decell and Odell [1966], Lewis and Odell [1966], Barten and Kloek [1965] and Schönfeld [1967]. The connection between the two solutions is discussed in paragraph six.

The last paragraph generalises a theorem of Rao. It gives the conditions for the equivalence of, on the one hand, best linear $P$-unbiased estimators with covariance matrix $I_t$, and, on the other hand, best linear $P$-unbiased estimators with covariance matrix $\Omega$ of any given rank.

## II.2 THE HYPOTHESES

The matrix form of the one-equation model is written as follows:

$$y = Xb + \varepsilon \tag{2.2.1}$$

in which:

$y$ is a $T \times 1$ vector of observations of the dependent variable;
$X$ is a $T \times k$ matrix of observations of the explanatory variables;
$b$ is a $k \times 1$ vector of unknown parameters;
$\varepsilon$ is a $T \times 1$ vector of error terms.

The following hypotheses are customary for this model:

*Hypothesis 1*

The vector $y$ of observations of the dependent variable and the matrix $X$ of observations of the non-stochastic explanatory variables are faultlessly observable.

The vector $\varepsilon$ of error terms is unobservable and has an expected value of zero.

Although economic variables are subject to observation errors, these are often negligible in comparison with the unobservable influences ($\varepsilon$) accompanying the dependent variable. The first part of this hypothesis can also be chosen as a starting point to describe economic reality. The second part of this hypothesis tells us something about the expected value of $\varepsilon$.

As is shown by Malinvaud [1966] this assumption is necessary as otherwise the model is not identifiable.

*Hypothesis 2*

The covariance matrix $\sigma^2\,\Omega$ of the vector $\varepsilon$ of error terms is non-singular.

In the classical model it is assumed that $\Omega = \sigma^2\,I_T$ or in other words: the error terms are uncorrelated and have all the same variance $\sigma^2$.

These assumptions, which simplify the problem considerably, are, however, not always in accordance with reality. It is, for instance, conceivable that the variance of the error terms increases when the values of the explanatory variables increase. Such a situation can be found in the studies on family budgets of Theil [1951] and Prais and Houthakker [1958]. The assumption of uncorrelated error terms will, especially when time series are used, not always be satisfied either. The influence of correlated error terms on the efficiency of the least-squares estimators was first examined by Cochrane and Orcutt [1949] and Orcutt and Cochrane [1949] and was exhaustively studied by Grenander [1954] and Rosenblatt [1956].

Suggestions for improvement of the least-squares method can be found in the works of, e.g., Klein [1953], Sargan [1964], Durbin [1960[a], 1960[b]], Malinvaud [1966] and Neeleman [1970].

When the covariance matrix is fully specified, these problems can easily be solved, as will be shown in the next paragraph. In practice, however, trying to specify this matrix causes many difficulties.

*Hypothesis 3*

The matrix $X$ of observations of the explanatory variables has rank $k$.

This hypothesis, viz. the absence of multicollinearity is also necessary for the identification of the model, as has been shown in I.4. In practice exact multicollinearity seldom occurs, but it often happens that the explanatory variables are nearly multicollinear.

In that case there are one or more approximately linear relationships between the explanatory variables, partly by chance, but also, in many cases, because of the fact that one or more variables depend on variables not included in the model. The consequences of multicollinearity in economic models have been examined by Winkler [1966] and Schilderinck [1970], to mention a few.

## II.3 THE (GENERALISED) LEAST-SQUARES ESTIMATORS

Let us take the linear model of the preceding paragraph.

$$y = Xb + \varepsilon \qquad (2.3.1)$$

and let us assume that the hypotheses 1 and 3 are valid. But, for the time being, we shall replace hypothesis 2 by the classical assumption, viz. that

$$E(\varepsilon\, \varepsilon') = \sigma^2 I_T \qquad (2.3.2)$$

The vector $b$ to be estimated is a fixed but unknown point in the $k$ dimensional parameter space $E_k$. The question is now how to construct a linear estimator

$$\hat{b} = Cy+c \tag{2.3.3}$$

of the vector $b$ so that:
1. this estimator is unbiased;
2. the variances of the elements of this estimator are minimal.

Such an estimator is called a best linear unbiased estimator.

As to 1. An estimator is called unbiased if

$$E(\hat{b}|b) = b \text{ for any } b \in E_k \tag{2.3.4}$$

i.e. the linear estimator $\hat{b} = Cy+c$ in consequence of (2.3.1), is unbiased if and only if:

$$\begin{cases} CX = I_k \\ c \;\;= 0 \end{cases} \tag{2.3.5}$$

As to 2. The variances to be minimized are found on the main diagonal of the matrix:

$$\begin{aligned} &E\{\hat{b}-E(\hat{b})\,|\,b\}\,\{\hat{b}-E(\hat{b})\,|\,b\}' \\ &\qquad = CE\{y-E(y)\}\,\{y-E(y)\}'\,C' = \sigma^2\,CC' \end{aligned} \tag{2.3.6}$$

so that the problem can be reduced to: Minimize the elements on the main diagonal of the matrix

$$CC' \tag{2.3.7}$$

under the constraint

$$CX = I_k \tag{2.3.8}$$

The following theorem is used to solve this problem.

*Theorem 2.3.9*

If $CX = I_k$, then

$$CC' = (X'X)^{-1}+\{C-(X'X)^{-1}X'\}\,\{C-(X'\,X)^{-1}X'\}' \tag{2.3.10}$$

*Proof*
This immediately follows from the right hand side of equation (2.3.10).

As all matrices in equation (2.3.10) are non-negative definite, they all have non-negative main diagonal elements so that from this the theorem immediately follows.

*Theorem 2.3.11*

The main diagonal elements of matrix $CC'$ are minimal under the constraint $CX = I_k$ if and only if $C = (X'X)^{-1} X'$.

From theorem 2.3.11 it follows, in consequence of (2.3.3) and (2.3.5) that

$$\hat{b} = (X'X)^{-1}X'y \tag{2.3.12}$$

is the best linear unbiased estimator of $b$. The covariance matrix of this estimator equals, in virtue of (2.3.6) and theorem 2.3.11:

$$\sigma^2 CC' = \sigma^2 (X'X)^{-1} \tag{2.3.13}$$

Let it be assumed that, for the model given by equation (2.3.1), hypotheses 1 up to and including 3 are valid, then:

$$E(\varepsilon\varepsilon') = \sigma^2 \Omega \tag{2.3.14}$$

in which $\Omega$ is non-singular.

As $\Omega$ is a symmetric, non-singular matrix there is a non-singular matrix $M$, so that:

$$M'\Omega M = I_T \tag{2.3.15}$$

Premultiplying equation (2.3.1) by matrix $M'$ yields:

$$M'y = M'Xb + M'\varepsilon \tag{2.3.16}$$

or

$$\bar{y} = \bar{X}b + \bar{\varepsilon} \tag{2.3.17}$$

in which:

$$\bar{y} = M'y \quad \bar{X} = M'X \quad \text{and} \quad \bar{\varepsilon} = M'\varepsilon \tag{2.3.18}$$

The model given by equation (2.3.17) now equals the model described above as, according to (2.3.14), (2.3.18) and (2.3.15), the following formula is valid:

$$E(\bar{\varepsilon}\bar{\varepsilon}') = \sigma^2 M'\Omega M = \sigma^2 I_T \tag{2.3.19}$$

but in that case the best linear unbiased estimator of $b$ is, according to (2.3.12) and (2.3.18):

$$\hat{b} = (\bar{X}'\bar{X})^{-1}\bar{X}'\bar{y} = (X'MM'X)^{-1}X'MM'y \tag{2.3.20}$$

or, taking into account that:

$$MM' = \Omega^{-1} \tag{2.3.21}$$

$$\hat{b} = (X'\Omega^{-1}X)^{-1}X'\Omega^{-1}y \tag{2.3.22}$$

The covariance matrix of this estimator equals, according to (2.3.13), (2.3.18) and (2.3.21):

$$\sigma^2 CC' = \sigma^2(\bar{X}'\bar{X})^{-1} = \sigma^2(X'\Omega^{-1}X)^{-1} \tag{2.3.23}$$

## II.4 BEST LINEAR UNBIASED ESTIMATORS OF ESTIMABLE FUNCTIONS

The difficulties arising when there is multicollinearity and the covariance matrix $\sigma^2\Omega$ has a rank smaller than $T$ will be solved in this paragraph in two steps.

First we shall consider the case in which the explanatory variables are exactly multicollinear whilst the covariance matrix is non-singular (part A); next we will deal with the case that the explanatory variables are exactly multicollinear whilst the covariance matrix is singular (part B).

Previous to this, however, we shall define the estimable function concept.

*Definition 2.4.1*

A parameter function $p'b$ is called an estimable function if there is a linear function $l'y$, so that

$$E(l'y) = p'b \text{ for any } b \in E_k. \tag{2.4.2}$$

With the aid of this definition it is easy to prove the following theorem:

*Theorem 2.4.3*

All linear parameter functions are estimable if and only if $R(X) = k$, in which $R(X)$ represents the rank of the matrix $X$.

*Proof*
If $R(X') = k$, the columns of $X'$ span a $k$-dimensional space. But in that case there is a vector $l$ for each $k$-dimensional vector $p$ so that $X'l = p$.

If $p'b$ is an estimable function, there is a vector $l$, by virtue of definition 2.4.1, so that $E(l'y) = p'b$. As $E(y) = Xb$, it follows that $X'l = p$. This $p$ belongs to the linear subspace spanned by the columns of $X'$. This is only true for any $p$ if $R(X') = k$.

From this theorem it immediately follows that in our case not all parameter functions are estimable, as only those parameter functions are estimable which satisfy $X'l = p$.

This means that a parameter function $p'b$ is only estimable if $p$ lies in the linear subspace spanned by the columns of $X'$.

## PART A

In this part we shall treat the case of multicollinearity between the explanatory variables, whilst the covariance matrix is of full rank.

For the sake of simplicity it is assumed that $\sigma^2 \Omega = \sigma^2 I_T$. As it is always possible to transform a model with a non-singular covariance matrix $\sigma^2 \Omega$ into a model with a unity matrix as covariance matrix with the aid of the transformation dealt with in the preceding paragraph.

*Theorem 2.4.4*

The best linear unbiased estimator of the estimable function $p'b$ is:

$$l^{*\prime}y \text{ with } l^* = X(X'X)^- p \tag{2.4.5}$$

in which $(X'X)^-$ represents a generalised inverse[1] of $X'X$.

*Proof*
The problem consists of minimizing the variance

$$V(l'y) = E[l'\{y - E(y)\}\{y - E(y)\}'l] = \sigma^2 l'l \tag{2.4.6}$$

under the constraint

$$E(l'y) = p'b \tag{2.4.7}$$

1. The concept of the generalised inverse of a matrix and its properties are treated in Appendix A.

As (2.4.7), by virtue of definition 2.4.1, is valid for any $b \in E_k$, this constraint can be written in the form of the following equation system.

$$X'l = p \tag{2.4.8}$$

As, moreover, the linear subspace spanned by the columns of $X'$ is the same as the one spanned by the columns of $X'X$ there is a $\lambda \in E_k$ so that:

$$(X'X)\lambda = p \tag{2.4.9}$$

With the aid of (2.4.5) and (2.4.9) we find

$$\begin{aligned} X'l^* &= (X'X)(X'X)^- p = (X'X)(X'X)^- (X'X)\lambda \\ &= (X'X)\lambda = p \end{aligned} \tag{2.4.10}$$

and

$$l^{*\prime} l^* = p'(X'X)^- (X'X)(X'X)^- p = p'(X'X)^- p \tag{2.4.11}$$

From (2.4.10) it follows, according to (2.4.8), that estimator $l^{*\prime}y$ is unbiased.

The only thing to be proved yet is that for any $l$ satisfying (2.4.7)

$$l'l \geq l^{*\prime} l^* \tag{2.4.12}$$

is valid.

This follows from the Cauchy-Schwarz inequality. For, in view of (2.4.5), (2.4.11) and (2.4.8) it immediately follows from:

$$\frac{(l'l^*)^2}{(l'l)(l^{*\prime}l^*)} \leqq 1 \tag{2.4.13}$$

that

$$l'l \geq \frac{(l'l^*)^2}{l^{*\prime}l^*} = \frac{\{l'X(X'X)^- p\}^2}{p'(X'X)^- p} = p'(X'X)^- p \tag{2.4.14}$$

With the aid of the transformation described in (2.3.16) up to and including (2.3.18), it follows from the above that, if the covariance matrix $\sigma^2 \Omega$ is not a diagonal one, the best linear unbiased estimator of $p'b$ will in view of (2.4.5) and (2.3.21), be equal to:

$$p'(\bar{X}'\bar{X})^- \bar{X}'\bar{y} = p'(X'\Omega^{-1}X)^- X'\Omega^{-1}y \tag{2.4.15}$$

and also that the variance of this estimator will, in view of (2.4.11) and (2.3.21), be equal to:

$$\sigma^2 p'(\bar{X}'\bar{X})^- p = \sigma^2 p'(X'\Omega^{-1}X)^- p \tag{2.4.16}$$

PART B

In this part it is assumed that there is multicollinearity among the explanatory variables and that the covariance matrix $\sigma^2 \Omega$ is singular.

For the sake of simplicity it is assumed that

$$\sigma^2 \Omega = \sigma^2 \begin{pmatrix} I_r & 0 \\ 0 & 0 \end{pmatrix} \tag{2.4.17}$$

The equivalent of theorem 2.4.4 will be in this case:

*Theorem 2.4.18*

The best linear unbiased estimator of the estimable function $p'b$ is:

$$l^{*\prime} y \text{ with } l^* = (X_1 D_1' + D_2')\, p \tag{2.4.19}$$

in which: $X_1$ is the matrix consisting of the first $r$ columns of $X$;
$X_2$ is the matrix consisting of the last $(T-r)$ columns of $X$.

$$\begin{pmatrix} D_1 & D_2 \\ D_3 & D_4 \end{pmatrix} \text{ is a generalised inverse of } \begin{pmatrix} X_1' X_1 & X_2' \\ X_2 & 0 \end{pmatrix} \tag{2.4.20}$$

*Proof*

Analogous to (2.4.8) a linear estimator of $p'b$ is unbiased if

$$l' X = p' \tag{2.4.21}$$

or in partitioned form

$$(X_1', X_2') \begin{pmatrix} l_1 \\ l_2 \end{pmatrix} = p \tag{2.4.22}$$

Taking into account (2.4.17), the variance of the estimator equals:

$$E(l' \varepsilon\varepsilon' l) = \sigma^2 l_1' l_1 \tag{2.4.23}$$

so that the problem consists of minimizing

$$l_1' l_1 \tag{2.4.24}$$

under the constraints

$$(X_1', X_2') \begin{pmatrix} l_1 \\ l_2 \end{pmatrix} = p \tag{2.4.25}$$

Equation (2.4.25) implies that there are variables: $m_1$ and $m_2$, so that

$$\begin{aligned} X_1' X_1 m_1 + X_2' m_2 &= p \\ X_2 m_1 &= 0 \end{aligned} \tag{2.4.26}$$

As the column vectors of $X_1'$ and $X_1'X_1$ span the same subspace, it follows that $p$ lies in the subspace spanned by the column vectors of $(X_1'X_1, X_2')$.

Let it be assumed that $R(X_1'X_1, X_2') = s \leq k$ and $R(X_2') = s_1 \leq s$, then the number of columns of $X_1'X_1$ independent of the columns of $X_2'$ equal $s - s_1 = s_2 \leq k - s_1$. From the second equation of (2.4.26) it follows that $m_1$ has to be orthogonal to the subspace spanned by the columns of $X_2'$. In view of the dimensions of $X_2'$, it follows that $k - s_1 \geq s_2$ elements of $m_1$ can be chosen freely. Together with the elements of $m_2$ this is enough to satisfy the first equation.

It is now easy to see that

$$l_1^* = X_1 D_1' p \qquad \text{and} \qquad l_2^* = D_2' p \tag{2.4.27}$$

satisfies the constraints (2.4.25), as according to (2.4.20), it follows from (2.4.26) that:

$$\begin{aligned} \begin{pmatrix} p \\ 0 \end{pmatrix} &= \begin{pmatrix} X_1'X_1 & X_2' \\ X_2 & 0 \end{pmatrix} \begin{pmatrix} D_1' & D_3' \\ D_2' & D_4' \end{pmatrix} \begin{pmatrix} X_1'X_1 & X_2' \\ X_2 & 0 \end{pmatrix} \begin{pmatrix} m_1 \\ m_2 \end{pmatrix} \\ &= \begin{pmatrix} X_1'X_1 & X_2' \\ X_2 & 0 \end{pmatrix} \begin{pmatrix} D_1' & D_3' \\ D_2' & D_4' \end{pmatrix} \begin{pmatrix} p \\ 0 \end{pmatrix} = \begin{pmatrix} X_1'X_1 & X_2' \\ X_2 & 0 \end{pmatrix} \begin{pmatrix} D_1' p \\ D_2' p \end{pmatrix} \end{aligned} \tag{2.4.28}$$

In view of (2.4.27) it follows from (2.4.28) that:

$$\begin{aligned} & X_1' X_1 D_1' p + X_2' D_2' p = X_1' l_1^* + X_2' l_2^* = p \\ & X_2 D_1' p = 0 \end{aligned} \tag{2.4.29}$$

With the aid of (2.4.27) and (2.4.29) we find

$$\begin{aligned} & l_1^{*\prime} l_1^* = p' D_1 X_1' l_1^* = p' D_1 p - p' D_1 X_2' l_2^* = p' D_1 p \\ & l_1^{*\prime} l_1 = p' D_1 X_1' l_1 = p' D_1 p - p' D_1 X_2' l_2 = p' D_1 p \end{aligned} \tag{2.4.30}$$

in which $l_1$ and $l_2$ are vectors satisfying (2.4.22).

By applying the Cauchy-Schwarz inequality to the vectors $l_1^*$ and $l_1$ in the same way as in (2.4.14) we find, in view of (2.4.30) that:

$$l_1' l_1 \geq \frac{(l_1^{*\prime} l_1)^2}{l_1^{*\prime} l_1^*} = p' D_1 p = l_1^{*\prime} l_1^* \tag{2.4.31}$$

In connection with (2.4.23) and (2.4.31), this means that

$$V(l' y) = \sigma^2 l_1' l_1 \geq \sigma^2 l_1^{*\prime} l_1^* = V(l^{*\prime} y) \tag{2.4.32}$$

in which, because of (2.4.27),

$$l^* = (X_1 D_1' + D_2') p \tag{2.4.33}$$

If $\sigma^2 \Omega$ is not of the form (2.4.17) but has rank $r$ it is still possible to use the foregoing results.

As $\Omega$ is symmetric there is a $T \times r$ matrix $M$ with rank $r$ so that

$$\Omega = MM' \tag{2.4.34}$$

The matrices $F$ and $N$ can now be chosen so that:

$$\begin{aligned} F' M &= I_r \\ \Omega N &= 0 \\ F' N &= 0 \\ N' N &= I_{T-r} \end{aligned} \tag{2.4.35}$$

Matrix $F$ has the property

$$FF' = \Omega^{-} \quad {}^{1)} \tag{2.4.36}$$

Conversion of the model (2.3.1) with the aid of the matrix $(F, N)'$ yields:

$$\bar{y} = \bar{X} b + \bar{\varepsilon} \tag{2.4.37}$$

in which:

$$\bar{y} = \begin{pmatrix} F' \\ N' \end{pmatrix} y \qquad \bar{X} = \begin{pmatrix} \bar{X}_1 \\ \bar{X}_2 \end{pmatrix} = \begin{pmatrix} F' \\ N' \end{pmatrix} X \qquad \bar{\varepsilon} = \begin{pmatrix} F' \\ N' \end{pmatrix} \varepsilon \tag{2.4.38}$$

The model given by equation (2.4.37) now equals the model that has been described above, as in consequence of (2.4.35) the following formula is valid:

$$E(\bar{\varepsilon}\bar{\varepsilon}') = \sigma^2 \begin{pmatrix} F' \\ N' \end{pmatrix} \Omega (F, N) = \sigma^2 \begin{pmatrix} I_r & 0 \\ 0 & 0 \end{pmatrix} \tag{2.4.39}$$

1. It even has the property $FF' = \Omega^{+}$. Also see II.5.

In view of (2.4.37), (2.4.19) and (2.4.36) the best linear unbiased estimator of $p'b$ equals in that case:

$$l^{*\prime} y = p'(\bar{D}_1 \bar{X}_1' + \bar{D}_2)\bar{y} = p'(\bar{D}_1 X' F + \bar{D}_2)\begin{pmatrix} F' \\ N' \end{pmatrix} y$$

$$= p'(\bar{D}_1 X' \Omega^- + \bar{D}_2 N')y \qquad (2.4.40)$$

in which

$$\begin{pmatrix} \bar{D}_1 & \bar{D}_2 \\ \bar{D}_3 & \bar{D}_4 \end{pmatrix}$$

represents a generalised inverse of

$$\begin{pmatrix} \bar{X}_1' \bar{X}_1 & \bar{X}_2' \\ \bar{X}_2 & 0 \end{pmatrix}$$

which in view of (2.4.36) and (2.4.38) equals:

$$\begin{pmatrix} X' \Omega^- X & X' N \\ N' X & 0 \end{pmatrix}$$

## II.5 BEST LINEAR $P$-UNBIASED ESTIMATORS

In this paragraph the so-called two-step method will be dealt with. The method provides a solution for the difficulties arising from the presence of exact multicollinearity of the explanatory variables and a singular covariance matrix.

The first step is to determine the class of estimators with minimum bias and the second step is to select, from this class, the estimator with minimum variance.

This is, in fact, Penrose's approach to the problem [1956]. The terminology used here comes from Chipman [1964].

From (2.3.5) we know that an estimator is unbiased if:

$$\begin{cases} CX = I_l \\ c \;\;\, = 0 \end{cases} \qquad (2.5.1)$$

If, however, the rank of $X$ is smaller than $k$, this condition cannot be satisfied.

An obvious approach, in this case, is to try somehow to minimize the bias arising from this.

An obvious procedure is to minimize

$$tr(I-CX)(I-CX)' \tag{2.5.2}$$

which equals the sum of the squares of the elements of matrix $(I-CX)$. It is easy to see that minimizing matrix

$$(I-CX)(I-CX)' \tag{2.5.3}$$

on the understanding that this means determining a matrix $C^*$ so that for any matrix $C$ it will be true that

$$(I-CX)(I-CX)' - (I-C^*X)(I-C^*X)' \tag{2.5.4}$$

is non-negative definite implies that (2.5.2) is a minimum as well, since, if $C = C^*$, the diagonal elements of (2.5.3) take an absolute minimum.

There is a simple solution to the problem posed in (2.5.3) as the following will show.

*Theorem 2.5.5*

A necessary and sufficient condition for

$$(I-CX)(I-CX)' \tag{2.5.6}$$

to be a minimum, is that $C$ satisfies the condition

$$CX = X^+X \tag{2.5.7}$$

in which $X^+$ represents the generalised Penrose inverse of matrix $X$.

*Proof*

From the fact that the rank of $X$ equals the rank of $X^+X$ it follows that there are matrices which satisfy (2.5.7).

According to (2.5.9) and the fact that $(I-X^+X)$ is idempotent it follows from

$$(I-CX) = (I-X^+X) + (X^+X-CX) \tag{2.5.8}$$

and

$$\left.\begin{aligned} X^+X(I-X^+X) &= X^+X - X^+XX^+X = 0 \\ CX(I-X^+X) &= CX - CX\,X^+X \quad\;\; = 0 \end{aligned}\right\} \tag{2.5.9}$$

that

$$
\begin{aligned}
(I-CX)(I-CX)' &= [(I-X^+X)+(X^+X-CX)] \\
&\quad \times [(I-X^+X)+(X^+X-CX)]' \\
&= (I-X^+X)(I-X^+X)+(I-X^+X)(X^+X-CX)' \\
&\quad +(X^+X-CX)(I-X^+X)+(X^+X-CX) \\
&\quad \times (X^+X-CX)' \\
&= (X^+X-CX)(X^+X-CX)'+(I-X^+X) \qquad (2.5.10)
\end{aligned}
$$

The second term on the right hand side of (2.5.10) is independent of $C$; the first term is symmetric, non-negative definite and equals the zero matrix if and only if $CX = X^+X$.

This proves the theorem.

From this theorem it follows that an estimator $\hat{b} = Cy$ in which a matrix $C$ satisfying (2.5.7), has minimum bias.

Such an estimator also possesses the following property: For any $b$ lying in the sub-space spanned by the column vectors of matrix $X^+$, the estimator $\hat{b} = Cy$ in which matrix $C$ satisfies (2.5.7), is an unbiased estimator of $b$, as in that case there is a vector $\lambda$ so that

$$b = X^+\lambda \qquad (2.5.11)$$

but, in view of (2.5.7) and (2.5.11), it follows that

$$E(\hat{b}) = CXb = X^+Xb = X^+XX^+\lambda = X^+\lambda = b \qquad (2.5.12)$$

Hence the following definition:

*Definition 2.5.13*

An estimator $\hat{b}$ of $b$ is called $P$-unbiased if

$$E(\hat{b}) = b \text{ for any } b \in \Gamma$$

in which

$$\Gamma = \{b \mid b = X^+\lambda \quad \text{for a} \quad \lambda \in E_T\}$$

Starting from this definition it is possible to develop the theory by proving that an estimator $\hat{b} = Cy$ is $P$-unbiased if and only if $CX = X^+X$. See for instance Schönfeld [1967].

In the remainder of this paragraph the estimators with minimum variance belonging to the class of $P$-unbiased estimators will be determined.

As in II.4 we shall distinguish two parts.

Part A refers to the case of exact multicollinearity between the explanatory variables and non-singular covariance matrix.

Part B deals with the case that the explanatory variables are exactly multicollinear whilst the covariance matrix is singular.

PART A

As in the preceding paragraph it is, in this part again assumed that $\sigma^2 \Omega = \sigma^2 I_T$, because, if this were not the case, it would always be possible – by means of the transformation described in II.3 – to rewrite the model in this form.

As was explained in (2.3.6) the covariance matrix of an estimator $\hat{b} = Cy$ equals, in that case:

$$E\{\hat{b}-E(\hat{b})|b\}\ \{\hat{b}-E(\hat{b})|b\}' = \sigma^2 CC' \tag{2.5.14}$$

The problem can now be formulated as follows:

Minimize the elements of the main-diagonal of matrix

$$CC' \tag{2.5.15}$$

under the constraint

$$CX = X^+X \tag{2.5.16}$$

*Theorem 2.5.17*

If $CX = X^+X$ then

$$CC' = X^+X^{+\prime} + (C-X^+)\,(C-X^+)' \tag{2.5.18}$$

*Proof*

From $X^+ = (X'X)^+X'$, it follows that

$$CX^{+\prime} = CX(X'X)^{+\prime} = X^+X(X'X)^{+\prime} = X^+X^{+\prime} = (X'X)^+X'X^{+\prime}$$
$$= (X'X)^+X'C' = X^+C' \tag{2.5.19}$$

Working out (2.5.18) with the aid of (2.5.19) we find

$$X^+X^{+\prime}+(C-X^+)\,(C-X^+)' = X^+X^{+\prime}+CC'-CX^{+\prime}$$
$$-X^+C'+X^+X^{+\prime} = CC'+2(X^+X^{+\prime}-CX^{+\prime}) = CC' \tag{2.5.20}$$

As all matrices in the equation are non-negative definite, they all have non-negative main-diagonal elements so that from this the theorem immediately follows.

*Theorem 2.5.21*

The main-diagonal elements of matrix $CC'$ are minimal under the constraint $CX = X^+X$, if and only if $C = X^+ = (X'X)^+X'$.

From theorem 2.5.21 it follows that

$$\hat{b} = (X'X)^+X'y \tag{2.5.22}$$

which is the best linear $P$-unbiased estimator of $b$.

In view of (2.5.14) the covariance matrix of this estimator equals:

$$\sigma^2CC' = \sigma^2(X'X)^+(X'X)(X'X)^+ = \sigma^2(X'X)^+ \tag{2.5.23}$$

If $\sigma^2\Omega$ is non-singular but different from $\sigma^2 I_T$, we find, with the aid of the transformation described in II.3 the model

$$\bar{y} = \bar{X}b + \bar{\varepsilon} \tag{2.5.24}$$

in which

$$\bar{y} = M'y,\ \bar{X} = M'X \text{ and } \bar{\varepsilon} = M'\varepsilon, \tag{2.5.25}$$

with the covariance matrix

$$E(\bar{\varepsilon}\bar{\varepsilon}') = \sigma^2 I_T \tag{2.5.26}$$

In this case the best linear $P$-unbiased estimator is – analogous to (2.5.22) – equal to:

$$\hat{b} = (\bar{X}'\bar{X})^+\bar{X}'\bar{y} = (X'MM'X)^+X'MM'y \tag{2.5.27}$$

or, since $MM' = \Omega^{-1}$:

$$\hat{b} = (X'\Omega^{-1}X)^+X'\Omega^{-1}y \tag{2.5.28}$$

The covariance matrix of this estimator equals in analogy with (2.5.23):

$$\sigma^2CC' = \sigma^2(\bar{X}'\bar{X})^+ = \sigma^2(X'\Omega^{-1}X)^+ \tag{2.5.29}$$

PART B

In this part it is assumed that there is multicollinearity among the explanatory variables and that the covariance matrix $\sigma^2\Omega$ is singular. For the sake of simplicity it is assumed that

$$\sigma^2 \Omega = \sigma^2 \begin{pmatrix} I_r & 0 \\ 0 & 0 \end{pmatrix} \tag{2.5.30}$$

as it is always possible to convert a model with a covariance matrix $\sigma^2 \Omega$ into a model with a covariance matrix of the form given by (2.5.30), with the aid of the conversion given in (2.4.35) and (2.4.38).

The equivalent of theorem (2.4.18) is:

*Theorem 2.5.31*

The best linear $P$-unbiased estimator of $b$ is:

$$\hat{b} = C_1 y_1 + C_2 y_2 \tag{2.5.32}$$

in which:

$$C_1 = [X_1(I_k - X_2^+ X_2)]^+ \tag{2.5.33}$$

$$C_2 = \{X^+ X - [X_1(I_k - X_2^+ X_2)]^+ X_1\} X_2^+ + Q(I_{T-r} - X_2 X_2^+) \tag{2.5.34}$$

in which

$y_1$ represents a vector consisting of the first $r$ elements of $y$;
$y_2$ represents a vector consisting of the last $T-r$ elements of $y$;
$Q$ represents any $k \times (T-r)$ matrix.

*Proof*
The proof of this theorem is based on Schönfeld [1967] but differs from it in details.

Analogous to part A the problem can be formulated as follows:

Minimize the main-diagonal elements of the covariance-matrix of the linear estimator $\hat{b} = Cy$

$$E[C(y-E(y))(y-E(y))' C'] = \sigma^2 C \begin{pmatrix} I_r & 0 \\ 0 & 0 \end{pmatrix} C' = \sigma^2 C_1 C_1' \tag{2.5.35}$$

under the constraint

$$CX = C_1 X_1 + C_2 X_2 = X^+ X \tag{2.5.36}$$

in which:

$C \;= (C_1, C_2)$;
$C_1$ represents a $k \times r$ matrix;
$C_2$ represents a $k \times T-r$ matrix.

By post-multiplication cf (2.5.36) by matrix $(I_k - X_2^+ X_2)$ the constraints on matrix $C_1$ are isolated.

In this case we find:

$$C_1 X_1 (I_k - X_2^+ X_2) + C_2 X_2 (I_k - X_2^+ X_2)$$
$$= C_1 X_1 (I_k - X_2^+ X_2) = X^+ X (I_k - X_2^+ X_2) \tag{2.5.37}$$

With the aid of Appendix A.52 it is possible to find a general solution to $C_2$ on the basis of (2.5.36).

This solution is

$$C_2 = (X^+ X - C_1 X_1) X_2^+ + Q(I_{T-r} - X_2 X_2^+) \tag{2.5.38}$$

in which $Q$ represents any $k \times (T-r)$ matrix.

The problem is, therefore, to minimize the main-diagonal elements of matrix $C_1 C_1'$, under constraint (2.5.37). $C_2$ can now be determined with the aid of (2.5.38).

$$X^+ X (I_k - X_2^+ X_2) = [X_1 (I_k - X_2^+ X_2)]^+ [X_1 (I_k - X_2^+ X_2)] \tag{2.5.39}$$

by virtue of Appendix A.30 so that it is obvious that according to theorem 2.5.21 $C_1$ is optimal if

$$C_1 = [X_1 (I_k - X_2^+ X_2)]^+ \tag{2.5.40}$$

In view of appendix A.14[d] the covariance matrix of this estimator equals:

$$\sigma^2 C_1 C_1' = \sigma^2 [X_1 (I_k - X_2^+ X_2)]^+ [X_1 (I_k - X_2^+ X_2)]^{+\prime}$$
$$= \sigma^2 [(I_k - X_2^+ X_2) X_1' X_1 (I_k - X_2^+ X_2)]^+ (I_k - X_2^+ X_2) \times$$
$$\times X_1' X_1 (I_k - X_2' X_2) [(I_k - X_2^+ X_2) X_1' X_1 (I_k - X_2^+ X_2)]^+$$
$$= \sigma^2 [(I_k - X_2^+ X_2) X_1' X_1 (I_k - X_2^+ X_2)]^+ \tag{2.5.41}$$

If the covariance matrix of $\varepsilon$ is not of the form (2.5.30) we will have to use the transformed model:

$$\bar{y} = \bar{X} b + \bar{\varepsilon} \tag{2.5.42}$$

which can be found with the aid of the transformation described in (2.4.35) and (2.4.38).

In that case the best linear $P$-unbiased estimator of $b$ will be:

$$\hat{b} = \bar{C}_1 \bar{y}_1 + \bar{C}_2 \bar{y}_2 \tag{2.5.43}$$

in which

$$\bar{C}_1 = [\bar{X}_1(I_k - \bar{X}_2^+ \bar{X}_2)]^+ = \{F'X[I_k-(N'X)^+ N'X]\}^+ \tag{2.5.44}$$

$$\begin{aligned}\bar{C}_2 &= [\bar{X}^+ \bar{X} - \bar{C}_1 \bar{X}_1]\bar{X}_2^+ + Q[I_{T-r} - \bar{X}_2 \bar{X}_2^+] \\ &= \{[X'(\Omega^+ + NN')X]^+ [X'(\Omega^+ + NN')X] \\ &\qquad - \bar{C}_1 F'X\} (N'X)^+ + Q[I_{T-r} - (N'X)(N'X)^+]\end{aligned} \tag{2.5.45}$$

$$\bar{y}_1 = F'y \tag{2.5.46}$$

$$\bar{y}_2 = N'y \tag{2.5.47}$$

In view of (2.4.36) the covariance matrix of this estimator will be:

$$\sigma^2 \bar{C}_1 \bar{C}_1' = \sigma^2 \{[I_k-(N'X)^+ N'X] X' \Omega^+ X[I_k-(N'X)^+ N'X]\}^+ \tag{2.5.48}$$

## II.6 THE RELATION BETWEEN BEST LINEAR $P$-UNBIASED ESTIMATORS AND ESTIMABLE FUNCTIONS

This paragraph deals with the relation between best linear $P$-unbiased estimators and best linear unbiased estimators of estimable functions.

*Theorem 2.6.1*

If $\hat{b} = Cy$ is a best linear $P$-unbiased estimator of $b$, then $p'\hat{b}$ is a best linear unbiased estimator of the estimable function $p'b$.

*Proof*

As to the estimators derived in part A of II.4 and II.5 this theorem follows immediately from the inspection of the formulae (2.4.5) and (2.5.22), and (2.4.15) and (2.5.28) respectively.

As to the case treated in part B of II.4 and II.5 this is not so obvious, which is clear when we compare the formulae (2.4.19) and (2.5.32).

So we have to prove that

$$p'C_1 y_1 + p'C_2 y_2 \tag{2.6.2}$$

in which $C_1$ and $C_2$ as defined in theorem (2.5.31), is a best linear unbiased estimator of the estimable function $p'b$.

From II.4 we know that determination of the best linear estimator $l'y$ of $p'b$ means minimalisation of the form

$$l_1' l_1 \tag{2.6.3}$$

under the constraint:

$$l_1' X_1 + l_2' X_2 = p' \tag{2.6.4}$$

To solve this problem we shall apply a method other than the one used in II.4. The problem is first transformed as follows:

Post-multiplication of (2.6.4) by matrix $(I_k - X_2^+ X_2)$ gives:

$$l_1' X_1 (I_k - X_2^+ X_2) = p'(I_k - X_2^+ X_2) \tag{2.6.5}$$

In view of Appendix A.43, $l_2$ of (2.6.4) equals:

$$l_2 = X_2'^+ p - X_2'^+ X_1' l_1 + I_{T-r} - (X_2 X_2^+) z_1 \tag{2.6.6}$$

in which $z_1$ represents any $(T-r)$ vector.

The problem is now to minimize $l_1' l_1$ under the constraint (2.6.5) and then to calculate $l_2$ with the aid of (2.6.6).

To solve the first part of this problem we rewrite (2.6.5) as follows:

$$l_1' A = p' A^+ A \tag{2.6.7}$$

in which:

$$A = X_1 (I_k - X_2^+ X_2)$$

As, in view of Appendix A.30

$$p' \{X_1 (I_k - X_2^+ X_2)\}^+ \{X_1 (I_k - X_2^+ X_2)\} = p' X^+ X (I_k - X_2^+ X_2) \tag{2.6.8}$$

and in view of the fact that $p'b$ is an estimable function so that $p'$ may be written as $\lambda' X$, it follows that

$$p' \{X_1 (I_k - X_2^+ X_2)\}^+ \{X_1 (I_k - X_2^+ X_2)\} = \lambda' X X^+ X \ (I_k - X_2^+ X_2)$$
$$= \lambda' X (I_k - X_2^+ X_2) = p'(I_k - X_2^+ X_2) \tag{2.6.9}$$

In view of appendix A.43, $l_1$ of (2.6.7) equals:

$$l_1 = (A^+)' p + (I_r - A A^+) z_2 \tag{2.6.10}$$

in which $z_2$ is any $r$-vector.

In view of Appendix A.4 up to and including A.7, substitution of (2.6.10) in (2.6.3) gives:

$$\begin{aligned} l_1' l_1 &= p' A^+ (A^+)' p + p' A^+ (I_r - AA^+) z_2 + \\ &\quad + z_2' (I_r - AA^+)' (A^+)' p + z_2' (I_r - AA^+)^+ (I_r - AA^+) z_2 \\ &= p' A^+ (A^+)' p + z_2' (I_r - AA^+) z_2 \end{aligned} \tag{2.6.11}$$

Since the two matrices $A^+ (A^+)'$ and $(I_r - AA^+)$ are non-negative definite, $l_1' l_1$ is minimum if $z_2$ is chosen so that:

$$(I_r - AA^+) z_2 = 0 \tag{2.6.12}$$

In view of the definition of $A$ given in (2.6.7), it follows that

$$l_1^{*\prime} = p' A^+ = p' \{X_1 (I_k - X_2^+ X_2)\}^+ \tag{2.6.13}$$

Substitution of $l_1^*$ in (2.6.6) gives:

$$l_2^{*\prime} = p' (I_k - A^+ X_1) X_2^+ + z_1' (I_{T-r} - X_2 X_2^+) \tag{2.6.14}$$

or, with the aid of Appendix A.33,

$$l_2^{*\prime} = p' (X^+ X - A^+ X_1) X_2^+ + z_1' (I_{T-r} - X_2 X_2^+) \tag{2.6.15}$$

Since $A^+ = C_1$ we find as the best linear unbiased estimator of $p' b$:

$$\begin{aligned} l_1^{*\prime} y_1 + l_2^{*\prime} y_2 &= p' \cdot C_1 y_1 + p' (X^+ X - C_1 X_1) X_2^+ y_2 \\ &\quad + z_1' (I_{T-r} - X_2 X_2') y_2 \end{aligned} \tag{2.6.16}$$

and in virtue of (2.5.34) this equals

$$l_1^{*\prime} y_1 + l_2^{*\prime} y_2 = p' C_1 y_1 + p' C_2 y_2 \tag{2.6.17}$$

which had to be proved.

## II.7 ON THE EQUIVALENCE OF BEST LINEAR $P$-UNBIASED ESTIMATORS

Before starting to derive the fundamental theorem treated in this paragraph, we shall first consider a procedure which, in simulation, is known as that of the 'control variates'. See, for instance, Tocher [1963] and Rao [1967], who uses the term 'covariance adjustment'.

The procedure is as follows:

Let it be assumed that $t_1$ and $t_2$ are two stochastic (vector) variables with $k_1$ and $k_2$ elements respectively. The expectations of these variables are:

$$\begin{cases} E(t_1) = \theta \\ E(t_2) = 0 \end{cases} \tag{2.7.1}$$

and their joint covariance matrix

$$E\begin{pmatrix} t_1 - \theta \\ t_2 \end{pmatrix}\begin{pmatrix} t_1 - \theta \\ t_2 \end{pmatrix}' = \begin{pmatrix} \Omega_{11} & \Omega_{12} \\ \Omega_{21} & \Omega_{22} \end{pmatrix} \tag{2.7.2}$$

Now take the stochastic variable

$$t_3 = t_1 - \Omega_{12}\,\Omega_{22}^{+}\,t_2 \tag{2.7.3}$$

The expectation of this variable is $\theta$ and its covariance matrix

$$\begin{aligned} E(t_3-\theta)(t_3-\theta)' &= E(t_1-\theta-\Omega_{12}\,\Omega_{22}^{+}\,t_2)(t_1-\vartheta-\Omega_{12}\,\Omega_{22}^{+}\,t_2)' \\ &= E(t_1-\theta)(t_1-\theta)' - E(t_1-\theta)\,t_2'\,\Omega_{22}^{+}\,\Omega_{21} - \Omega_{12}\,\Omega_{22}^{+}\,Et_2(t_1-\theta)' + \\ &\quad + \Omega_{12}\,\Omega_{22}^{+}\,E(t_2\,t_2')\,\Omega_{22}^{+}\,\Omega_{21} = \Omega_{11} - \Omega_{12}\,\Omega_{22}^{+}\,\Omega_{21} \end{aligned} \tag{2.7.4}$$

From (2.7.4) it follows that

$$E(t_1-\theta)(t_1-\theta)' - E(t_3-\theta)(t_3-\theta)' = \Omega_{12}\,\Omega_{22}^{+}\,\Omega_{21} \tag{2.7.5}$$

Since $\Omega_{22}$ is non-negative definite, $\Omega_{22}^{+}$ and $\Omega_{12}\ \Omega_{22}^{+}\ \Omega_{21}$, too, are non-negative definite. But in this case, all terms on the main-diagonal are larger than or equal to zero.

From this it follows that the variances belonging to the elements of $t_3$ are smaller than or equal to the variances of the corresponding elements of $t_1$.

A necessary and sufficient condition for the above-sketched procedure to produce no variable with smaller variances, is that $\Omega_{12} = 0$.

That this condition is sufficient follows immediately from (6.7.3), whilst its necessity can be demonstrated as follows.

Let it be assumed that $\Omega_{22}$ is non-singular and, consequently, positive definite. Then $\Omega_{22}^{+} = \Omega_{22}^{-1}$ will also be positive definite. From this it follows immediately that the terms on the main-diagonal can only be zero if $\Omega_{12} = 0$.

Let it be assumed that $\Omega_{22}$ is singular and that $R(\Omega_{22}) = r < k_2$. Then, with probability one, there are $(k_2 - r)$ elements of $t_2$ which are linear combinations of the remaining $r$ elements.

It can be said, without loss of generality, that the latter are the first $r$ elements of $t_2$. Let the vector consisting of these elements be called $t_2^*$. The covariance matrix of $t_2^*$ is non-singular so that it follows from the above that there is no variable with smaller variances if

$$E(t_1-\theta)(t_2^*)' = \Omega_{12}^* = 0 \tag{2.7.6}$$

But in this case $\Omega_{12}=0$ as well, since the last $(k_2-r)$ elements are, with probability one, linear combinations of the remaining elements.

*Theorem 2.7.7*

A necessary and sufficient condition for the best linear $P$-unbiased estimator with covariance matrix $\Omega$ of arbitrary rank to be equivalent to the best linear $P$-unbiased estimator with covariance matrix $\sigma^2 I_T$, is that $X'\Omega Z=0$; in which $R(X)=r$ and $Z$ is a $T\times(T-r)$ matrix with $R(Z)=T-r$, so that $Z'X=0$.

*Proof*
If the covariance matrix of $\varepsilon$ equals $\sigma^2 I_T$, the best linear $P$-unbiased estimator of $b$ is, in virtue of (2.5.22), equal to

$$\hat{b} = (X'X)^+X'y \tag{2.7.8}$$

According to definition (2.5.13) this estimator is also $P$-unbiased if the covariance matrix of $\varepsilon$ equals $\Omega \neq \sigma^2 I_T$, since, if $b$ lies in the subspace spanned by the columns of $X^+$, there is a $\lambda$ so that $b=X^+\lambda$.

But then, in view of Appendix A.14[e]

$$E(\hat{b}) = (X'X)^+X'Xb = (X'X)^+X'XX^+\lambda = X^+XX^+\lambda = X^+\lambda = b \tag{2.7.9}$$

In view of (2.7.2) and (2.7.8), the covariance matrix of $t_1$ and $t_2$ with $t_1=\hat{b}$ and $t_2=Z'y$ is equal to

$$\Omega_{12} = E[\hat{b}-E(\hat{b})][y-E(y)]'Z = E\{(X'X)^+X'[y-E(y)]\times \times[y-E(y)]'Z\} = (X'X)^+X'\Omega Z \tag{2.7.10}$$

Now, $\Omega_{12}=0$ if and only if $X'\Omega Z=0$.

The necessity of this condition follows immediately when we consider (2.7.10). That this condition is also required can be shown as follows.

Let it be assumed that

$$(X'X)^+X'\Omega Z = X^+\Omega Z = 0 \tag{2.7.11}$$

then it also follows that

$$X'XX^{+}\Omega Z = X'(X^{+})'X'\Omega Z = X'(X')^{+}X'\Omega Z = X'\Omega Z = 0 \quad (2.7.12)$$

Therefore, the variance-reducing method described in (2.7.3) yields, when $t_2 = Z'y$, no estimator of $b$ with a smaller variance if $X'\Omega Z = 0$. In virtue of the data provided by this theorem $X'Z = 0$, whilst the column vectors of $Z$ form the basis of a subspace perpendicular to the subspace spanned by the column vectors of $X$, and, as the column vectors of $(X, Z)$ span the whole $T$-dimensional space, every linear function of $y$ with expectation zero can be written as $l'Zy$.

But from this it follows that, if $X'\Omega Z = 0$, there is no vector $t_2$ with expectation zero by means of which it would be possible to reduce the variance of $\hat{b}$.

# III. Estimation of a model consisting of several equations

## III.1 INTRODUCTION

This chapter deals with estimation of the reduced form and the structural form of the simultaneous equations model.

The second part deals with the classical hypotheses underlying this model.

The third part shows that for the reduced form, the normal least-squares method produces the best linear unbiased estimators for the reduced form coefficients, even if the covariance matrix is singular.

The requirement of the classical hypotheses that this matrix should be non-singular can be disregarded for the reduced form estimation.

Disregarding the hypothesis that explanatory variables should not be multicollinear, it is very easy to show that the best linear *P*-unbiased estimators of the reduced form coefficients are also independent of the covariance matrix, and here again, therefore, the form of this matrix is of no importance.

The fourth shows, with the aid of some well-known theorems on the extremes of quadratic forms, a new derivation of the *k*-class estimators of the structural form coefficients. This has the advantage of allowing a choice, at the end of the derivation, of the normalisation rule one wishes to apply. From these *k*-class estimators, an asymptotic property is derived in part 5, especially of the two-stage least-squares estimators and the limited-information maximum-likelihood estimators belonging to this class.

The sixth part studies the way in which multicollinearity may occur in both estimation methods. This study is based on Klein and Nakamura [1962]. The properties given in part 6 imply a preference for the two-stage least-squares estimators.

Finally, part 7 shows a method of generalising the two-stage least-squares estimators in the case of multicollinearity.

Lastly, an asymptotic property of these estimators is derived.

## III.2 THE HYPOTHESES

The estimation methods discussed in this part proceed from a number of hypotheses some of which are generalisations of the hypotheses for the single-equation model discussed in II.2.

Written as a matrix, the simultaneous-equations model has the following form:

$$B'y_t + C'x_t = \varepsilon_t \qquad (T1, 2, \ldots, T) \tag{3.2.1}$$

in which:

- $y_t$ represents the vector of observations of the $m$ dependent variables at moment $t$.
- $x_t$ represents the vector of observations of the $k$ explanatory variables at moment $t$.
- $B'$ represents an $m \times m$ matrix of unknown parameters.
- $C'$ represents an $m \times k$ matrix of unknown parameters.
- $\varepsilon_t$ represents the vector of random errors at moment $t$.

The following assumptions are customary for this model.

*Hypothesis 1*

The vector $y_t$ of observations of the dependent variables and vector $x_t$ of the observations of the non-stochastic explanatory variables can be faultlessly observed.

The vector $\varepsilon_t$ of error-terms cannot be observed and has an expectation of zero.

This hypothesis is the generalisation of the corresponding hypothesis 1 from chapter II.

*Hypothesis 2*

The $\varepsilon_t$ are mutually independent identically distributed stochastic variables with a non-singular variance-covariance matrix $\sigma^2 \Sigma$.

This hypothesis is the generalisation of a special hypothesis 2 from Chapter II. The case of $\Omega = \sigma^2 I_T$ was mentioned there in the comment on this hypothesis, i.e. the error-terms are stochastically independent or uncorrelated at different moments. Hypothesis 2 assumes that the error-terms are stochastically independent at different moments. Here again, situations are conceivable in which this assumption is not realistic. Suggestions for improving existing estimation methods are found, for instance, in Sargan [1961], Amemya [1966], Hendry [1969], Wickens [1969] and Fair [1970] and, if $B$ is a unity matrix, in Parks [1967] and Kmenta and Gilbert [1970].

*Hypothesis 3*

The $T \times k$ matrix $X$ of observations of the $k$-explanatory variables has the rank $k$.

This hypothesis is also a generalisation of the corresponding hypothesis from the last chapter.

The consequences of multicollinearity have been described by Klein and Nakamura [1962] and Winkler [1966].

Suggestions for improving existing estimation methods have been made by Kloek and Mennes [1960] and, if $B$ is a unity matrix, by Plasmans [1970].

*Hypothesis 4*

The model is complete, which means: $B^{-1}$ exists.

*Hypothesis 5*

The equations to be estimated are identified.

The following hypotheses are now introduced for the estimation method in order to derive an asymptotic property therefrom. This property, the consistency of certain estimators, plays a large part in a model consisting of a number of equations, as small sample properties cannot usually be derived. This is in contrast to the model consisting of one equation whose small sample properties are known.

*Hypothesis 6*

The vectors $x_t$ are uniformly bounded.

*Hypothesis 7*

$$\lim_{T \to \infty} \frac{1}{T} X'X \quad \text{exists and is non-singular.}$$

The latter hypothesis represents the equivalent of hypothesis 3; for it follows from hypothesis 3 that matrix $X'X$ has the rank $k$ and from hypothesis 7 that this remains so even if there is an unlimited increase in the number of observations.

The reduced form of the model is:

$$y_t = \pi' x_t + \eta_t \tag{3.3.1}$$

in which:

$$\begin{cases} \pi' = -(B')^{-1} C' \\ \eta_t = \quad (B')^{-1} \varepsilon_t \end{cases} \tag{3.3.2}$$

It clearly follows from hypotheses 1 and 2 that:

1. The expectation of the vector $\eta_t$ equals zero and is independent of the explanatory variables.
2. The $\eta_t$ are mutually independent, identically distributed stochastic variables with a non-singular covariance matrix.

$$\sigma^2 \Omega = \sigma^2 (B^{-1})' \Sigma B^{-1}$$

We can now write (3.3.1) as:

$$Y = X\pi + \eta \tag{3.3.3}$$

in which:

$$Y = \begin{pmatrix} y_1' \\ \vdots \\ y_T' \end{pmatrix}, \quad X = \begin{pmatrix} x_1' \\ \vdots \\ x_T' \end{pmatrix}, \quad \eta = \begin{pmatrix} \eta_1' \\ \vdots \\ \eta_T' \end{pmatrix} \tag{3.3.4}$$

With the aid of the Kronecker product for matrices, (3.3.3) can be re-written as:

$$\operatorname{vec} Y = (I_m \otimes X) \operatorname{vec} \pi + \operatorname{vec} \eta \tag{3.3.5}$$

in which vec $Y$, vec $\pi$ and vec $\eta$ are the vectors formed when the columns of matrices $Y$, $\pi$ and $\eta$ respectively are placed one underneath the other.

The properties of the Kronecker product for matrices used throughout the present chapter are given in Appendix B.

Changing (3.3.1) to (3.3.5) alters the model consisting of several equations into a model consisting of one equation only, and the theory evolved in chapter II can therefore be applied.

As the covariance matrix of vec $\eta$ equals:

$$\sigma^2 (\Omega \otimes I_T) \tag{3.3.6}$$

the best linear unbiased estimator of vec $\pi$ is found to be:

$$\begin{aligned} \operatorname{vec} \hat{\pi} &= [(I_m \otimes X')(\Omega^{-1} \otimes I_T)(I_m \otimes X)]^{-1} (I_m \otimes X')(\Omega^{-1} \otimes I_T) \operatorname{vec} Y \\ &= [I_m \otimes (X'X)^{-1} X'] \operatorname{vec} Y \end{aligned} \tag{3.3.7}$$

with the covariance matrix:

$$\sigma^2[(I_m \otimes X)'(\Omega^{-1} \otimes I_T)(I_m \otimes X)]^{-1} = \sigma^2[\Omega \otimes (X'X)^{-1}] \tag{3.3.8}$$

Re-writing (3.3.7) as:

$$\hat{\pi} = (X'X)^{-1}X'Y \tag{3.3.9}$$

shows that the best linear unbiased estimators of vec $\pi$ are the ordinary least squares estimators.

It is easy to show with theorem 2.7.7 that the ordinary least squares estimators are best linear and unbiased when $\Omega$ is singular.

On the assumption that $Z$ is a matrix of maximum rank so that $X'Z=0$, then:

$$(I_m \otimes X')(I_m \otimes Z) = (I_m \otimes X'Z) = 0 \tag{3.3.10}$$

and:

$$(I_m \otimes X')(\Omega \otimes I_T)(I_m \otimes Z) = (\Omega \otimes X'Z) = 0 \tag{3.3.11}$$

and, according to the above-mentioned theorem, the ordinary least squares estimators are then best linear and unbiased.

With the aid of the same theorem it can similarly be shown that – if hypothesis 3 was not fulfilled – the best linear $P$ unbiased estimator of vec $\pi$ equals:

$$\begin{aligned} \text{vec}\,\hat{\pi} &= [(I_m \otimes X')(I_m \otimes X)]^+(I_m \otimes X)'\,\text{vec}\,Y \\ &= [I_m \otimes (X'X)^+X']\,\text{vec}\,Y \end{aligned} \tag{3.3.12}$$

with the covariance matrix:

$$\begin{aligned} &E\{[I_m \otimes (X'X)^+X'][\text{vec}\,Y - E(\text{vec}\,Y)][\text{vec}\,Y - E(\text{vec}\,Y)]'\times \\ &\quad \times [I_m \otimes X(X'X)^+]\} = \sigma^2[I_m \otimes (X'X)^+X'](\Omega \otimes I_T)\times \\ &\quad \times [I_m \otimes (X'X)^+X']' = \sigma^2[\Omega \otimes (X'X)^+] \end{aligned} \tag{3.3.13}$$

## III.4 THE $k$-CLASS ESTIMATORS

The last section showed how the parameters of the reduced form of the model might be estimated. The present section will derive a class of estimators for the parameters of the structural form of the model. This class of estimators, known as $k$-class estimators, was found by Theil [1961] somewhat heuristically. A theoretically satisfactory derivation was later given by Malinvaud [1966] and was afterwards corrected on some points by Neeleman [1970]. It is as follows:

Assuming that the first equation of the model is to be estimated. Without altering the generality of the conclusions it can be said that the number of dependent variables in this equation is $m$. Based on the order-condition for identification, it can be said that this equation will be identifiable only if the number of explanatory variables not appearing in the equations is at least $(m-1)$, so that the first row of matrix $C'$ contains at least $(m-1)$ zeros.

If the variables are arranged so that these zeros occupy the last places of the first row of $C'$, the first equation of the structural form can be written:

$$b'y_t + (c', 0)x_t = \varepsilon_t \qquad (t = 1, 2, \ldots, T) \qquad (3.4.1)$$

in which:

$b'$ represents the first $B'$ row
$(c'0)$ represents the first $C'$ row

As the ordinary least-squares estimators of $b$ and $c$ are not unbiased and not even asymptotically efficient, another estimation method will have to be sought.

Let us therefore start with the reduced form of the model:

$$\text{vec}\, Y = (I_m \otimes X)\, \text{vec}\, \pi + \text{vec}\, \eta \qquad (3.4.2)$$

We try to estimate this by taking into account the condition:

$$\pi b = \begin{pmatrix} -c \\ 0 \end{pmatrix} \qquad (3.4.3)$$

or, re-written with the Kronecker product for matrices:

$$(b' \otimes I_k)\, \text{vec}\, \pi = \begin{pmatrix} -c \\ 0 \end{pmatrix} \qquad (3.4.4)$$

This problem might be solved if vectors $b$ and $c$ were known but it is these that have to be estimated. The following solution is the logical result.

*Step 1*

Define the best linear unbiased estimator of vec $\pi$ starting with a known $b$ and $c$ and allowing for the side condition (3.4.4).

*Step 2*

With the aid of the estimator found in Step 1, calculate the estimator of $\sigma^2$. This is a function of $b$ and $c$. Next calculate the values of $b$ and $c$ for which this estimator of $\sigma^2$ is the minimum.

These steps will be dealt with in detail in the sequel.

*Re Step 1*

This problem can be solved as follows. With the aid of the transformation discussed in II.3, the model (3.4.2) can be converted to:

$$(M' \otimes I_T) \operatorname{vec} Y = (M' \otimes X) \operatorname{vec} \pi + (M' \otimes I_T) \operatorname{vec} \eta \tag{3.4.5}$$

in which $M$ represents a matrix that should be chosen in such a way that the covariance matrix of $(M' \otimes I_T) \operatorname{vec} \eta$ equals:

$$\sigma^2 (M' \otimes I_T)(\Omega \otimes I_T)(M \otimes I_T) = \sigma^2 (M'\Omega M \otimes I_T) = \sigma^2 (I_m \otimes I_T) \tag{3.4.6}$$

The problem is to define an estimator as follows in the class of linear estimators, analogously to (2.3.3) and taking into account (2.3.18):

$$\operatorname{vec} \hat{\pi} = C(M' \otimes I_T) \operatorname{vec} Y + d \tag{3.4.7}$$

so that:

$$E(\operatorname{vec} \hat{\pi}) = C(M' \otimes X) \operatorname{vec} \pi + d = \operatorname{vec} \pi \tag{3.4.8}$$

subject to the side condition (3.4.4).

Let us rewrite (3.4.8) as:

$$[C(M' \otimes X) - I_{mk}] \operatorname{vec} \pi + d = 0 \tag{3.4.9}$$

and, taking into account appendix A.43, (3.4.4) as:

$$\operatorname{vec} \pi = (b' \otimes I_k)^+ \begin{pmatrix} -c \\ 0 \end{pmatrix} + [I_{mk} - (bb^+ \otimes I_k)]\, e \tag{3.4.10}$$

in which $e$ represents an arbitrarily chosen $(mk)$ vector. Substitution of (3.4.10) into (3.4.9) gives:

$$[C(M' \otimes X) - I_{mk}] \left\{ (b' \otimes I_k)^+ \begin{pmatrix} -c \\ 0 \end{pmatrix} + [I_{mk} - (bb^+ \otimes I_k)]\, e \right\} + d = 0 \tag{3.4.11}$$

It follows from this that for an unbiased estimator $C$ and $d$ must be chosen so as to satisfy:

$$\begin{cases} [C(M' \otimes X)-I_{mk}][I_{mk}-(bb^{+} \otimes I_k)] = 0 & (3.4.12) \\ d = [C(M' \otimes X)-I_{mk}](b' \otimes I_k)^{+} \begin{pmatrix} c \\ 0 \end{pmatrix} & (3.4.13) \end{cases}$$

Reviewing (3.4.7) and (3.4.13) shows us that the choice of the estimator is determined by the choice of $C$; for from (3.4.13) we see that $d$ is directly dependent on $C$.

Now (3.4.12) may be rewritten as:

$$C(M' \otimes X)[I_{mk}-(bb^{+} \otimes I_k)] = [I_{mk}-(bb^{+} \otimes I_k)] \tag{3.4.14}$$

Taking into account the fact that:
- the right-hand term of (3.4.14) is an idempotent matrix
- in view of (2.3.21) $\Omega MM' = I_m$
- $X^{+}X = I_k$

the right-hand term of (3.4.14) can be written:

$$\begin{aligned} &[I_{mk}-(bb^{+} \otimes I_k)] = (\Omega MM' \otimes X^{+}X)[I_{mk}-(bb^{+} \otimes I_k)] \\ &= (\Omega M \otimes X^{+})(M' \otimes X)[I_{mk}-(bb^{+} \otimes I_k)] \\ &= (\Omega M \otimes M^{+})\{(M' \otimes X)[I_{mk}-(bb^{+} \otimes I_k)]\} \times \\ &\quad \times \{(M' \otimes X)[I_{mk}-(bb^{+} \otimes I_k)]\}^{+}\{(M' \otimes X)[I_{mk}-(bb^{+} \otimes I_k)]\} \\ &= [I_{mk}-(bb^{+} \otimes I_k)]\{(M' \otimes X)[I_{mk}-(bb^{+} \otimes I_k)]\}^{+} \times \\ &\quad \times \{(M' \otimes X)[I_{mk}-(bb^{+} \otimes I_k)]\} \\ &= \{(M' \otimes X)[I_{mk}-(bb^{+} \otimes I_k)]\}^{+} \times \\ &\quad \times \{(M' \otimes X)[I_{mk}-(bb^{+} \otimes I_k)]\}[I_{mk}-(bb^{+} \otimes I_k)] \\ &= \{(M' \otimes X)[I_{mk}-(bb^{+} \otimes I_k)]\}^{+}\{(M' \otimes X)[I_{mk}-(bb^{+} \otimes I_k)]\} \end{aligned} \tag{3.4.15}$$

The problem then becomes:

Minimize the terms on the main diagonal of

$$CC' \tag{3.4.16}$$

with the side condition (3.4.14) which, in view of (3.4.15), can be written:

$$\begin{aligned} C(M' \otimes X)[I_{mk}-(bb^{+} \otimes I_k)] &= \{(M' \otimes X)[I_{mk}-(bb^{+} \otimes I_k)]\}^{+} \times \\ &\quad \times \{(M' \otimes X)[I_{mk}-(bb^{+} \otimes I_k)]\} \end{aligned} \tag{3.4.17}$$

This problem has already been solved in theorem 2.5.21, application of which gives:

$$C = \{(M' \otimes X)[I_{mk} - (bb^{+} \otimes I_k)]\}^{+} \tag{3.4.18}$$

Since the right-hand term of (3.4.18), with the aid of appendix A.40, can be written:

$$(M' \otimes X)^{+} \{I_{mk} - [(b' \otimes I_k)(M' \otimes X)^{+}]^{+} [(b' \otimes I_k)(M' \otimes X)^{+}]\} \tag{3.4.19}$$

we find the estimator, taking into account (3.4.7), (3.4.9) and (3.4.13), to be:

$$\begin{aligned} \text{vec}\, \hat{\pi} = {} & (M' \otimes X)^{+} \{I_{mk} - [(b' \otimes I_k)(M' \otimes X)^{+}]^{+} \times \\ & \times [(b' \otimes I_k)(M' \otimes X)^{+}]\} (M' \otimes I_T) \text{ vec } Y + [(M' \otimes X)^{+} \times \\ & \times \{I_{mk} - [(b' \otimes I_k)(M' \otimes X)^{+}]^{+} [(b' \otimes I_k)(M' \otimes X)^{+}]\} \times \\ & \times (M' \otimes X) - I_{mk}] \cdot (b' \otimes I_k)^{+} \begin{pmatrix} c \\ 0 \end{pmatrix} \end{aligned} \tag{3.4.20}$$

Since:

- in view of (2.3.21) $(M^{-1})' M^{-1} = \Omega$
- $X^{+}X = I_k$
- $(M' \otimes X)^{+} = [(M^{-1})' \otimes X^{+}]$

then:

$$\begin{aligned} & [(b' \otimes I_k)(M' \otimes X)^{+}]^{+} [(b' \otimes I_k)(M' \otimes X)^{+}] \\ & = [b'(\quad{}^{-1})' \otimes X^{+}]^{+} [b'(M^{-1})' X^{+}] \\ & = [(M^{-1}b)^{+\prime} b'(\quad{}^{-1})' \otimes XX^{+}] \\ & = [(b' \Omega b)^{-1} M^{-1} bb'(M^{-1})' \otimes XX^{+}] \end{aligned} \tag{3.4.21}$$

may furthermore be simplified with the aid of (3.4.20) to

$$\begin{aligned} \text{vec}\, \hat{\pi} & = (I_m \otimes X^{+}) \text{ vec } Y - [(b' \Omega b)^{-1} (M^{-1}) bb' \otimes X^{+}] \text{ vec } Y + \\ & + [I_{mk} - \{(b' \Omega b)^{-1} (M^{-1})' M^{-1} bb' \otimes I_k\} - I_{mk}] [b(b'b)^{-1} \otimes I_k] \begin{pmatrix} c \\ 0 \end{pmatrix} \\ & = (I_m \otimes X^{+}) \text{ vec } Y - [(b' \Omega b)^{-1} \Omega bb' \otimes X^{+}] \times \\ & \quad \times \text{vec } Y - [(b' \Omega b)^{-1} \Omega b \otimes I_k] \begin{pmatrix} c \\ 0 \end{pmatrix} \end{aligned} \tag{3.4.22}$$

*Re Step 2*

Proceeding from model (3.4.6), we use for the estimator of $\sigma^2$ that had to be minimized, the well-known least-squares estimator.

Apart from a constant, this estimator equals:

$$S = [(M' \otimes I_T) \text{ vec } Y - (M' \otimes X) \text{ vec } \hat{\pi}]' \times$$
$$\times [(M' \otimes I_T) \text{ vec } Y - (M' \otimes X) \text{ vec } \hat{\pi}] \tag{3.4.23}$$

Taking into account (2.3.21), substitution of (3.4.22) into (3.4.23) gives:

$$\begin{aligned}
S &= (\text{vec } Y)'(M \otimes I_T)(M' \otimes I_T) \text{ vec } Y - 2(\text{vec } Y)'(M \otimes I_T) \times \\
&\quad \times (M' \otimes X) \text{ vec } \hat{\pi} + (\text{vec } \hat{\pi})'(M \otimes X')(M' \otimes X) \text{ vec } \hat{\pi} \\
&= (\text{vec } Y)'(\Omega^{-1} \otimes I_T) \text{ vec } Y - 2(\text{vec } Y)'(\Omega^{-1} \otimes XX^+) \text{ vec } Y + \\
&\quad + 2(\text{vec } Y)'[(b'\Omega b)^{-1} bb' \otimes XX^+] \text{ vec } Y + \\
&\quad + 2(\text{vec } Y)'[(b'\Omega b)^{-1} b \otimes X] \begin{pmatrix} c \\ 0 \end{pmatrix} + (\text{vec } Y)'(\Omega^{-1} \otimes XX^+) \times \\
&\quad \times \text{vec } Y - 2(\text{vec } Y)'[(b'\Omega b)^{-1} bb' \otimes XX^+] \times \\
&\quad \times \text{vec } Y - 2(\text{vec } Y)'[(b'\Omega b)^{-1} b \otimes X] \begin{pmatrix} c \\ 0 \end{pmatrix} + \\
&\quad + (\text{vec } Y)'[(b'\Omega b)^{-1} bb' \otimes XX^+] \text{ vec } Y + 2(\text{vec } Y)' \times \\
&\quad \times [(b'\Omega b)^{-1} b \otimes X] \begin{pmatrix} c \\ 0 \end{pmatrix} + (c', 0)[(b'\Omega b)^{-1} \otimes X'X] \begin{pmatrix} c \\ 0 \end{pmatrix} \\
&= (\text{vec } Y)'(\Omega^{-1} \otimes I_T) \text{ vec } Y - (\text{vec } Y)'(\Omega^{-1} \otimes XX^+) \text{ vec } Y + \\
&\quad + (\text{vec } Y)'[(b'\Omega b)^{-1} bb' \otimes XX^+] \text{ vec } Y + 2(\text{vec } Y)' \times \\
&\quad \times [(b'\Omega b)^{-1} b \otimes X] \begin{pmatrix} c \\ 0 \end{pmatrix} + (c', 0)[(b'\Omega b)^{-1} \otimes X'X] \begin{pmatrix} c \\ 0 \end{pmatrix}
\end{aligned} \tag{3.4.24}$$

in which $b$ and $c$ should be chosen so that $S$ will have the minimum value.

This means that we can confine ourselves to the part of $S$ containing $b$ and $c$, which can be written:

$$\frac{(\text{vec } Y)'(bb' \otimes XX^+) \text{ vec } Y + 2(\text{vec } Y)'(b \otimes X_1)c + c'(1 \otimes X_1'X_1)c}{b'\Omega b} \tag{3.4.25}$$

in which $X_1$ is the matrix consisting of the first $k_1$ columns of $X$ ($k_1$ is the number of explanatory variables belonging to the first equation).

The form (3.4.25) can now be written:

$$\frac{[v-(1\otimes X_1)c]'[v-(1\otimes X_1)c]}{b'\Omega b} \tag{3.4.26}$$

with:

$$v = -(b'\otimes XX^+) \text{ vec } Y \tag{3.4.27}$$

According to the theory of least squares the numerator of (3.4.26), as a function of $C$, is the minimum when:

$$\begin{aligned}\hat{c} &= [(1\otimes X_1)'(1\otimes X_1)]^{-1}(1\otimes X_1)'v \\ &= -[1\otimes(X_1'X_1)^{-1}X_1'][b'\otimes XX^+] \text{ vec } Y \\ &= -(b'\otimes X_1^+XX^+) \text{ vec } Y = -[b'\otimes X_1^+] \text{ vec } Y\end{aligned} \tag{3.4.28}$$

Substitution of (3.4.28) into (3.4.25) reduces the problem to one of minimising the function:

$$\begin{aligned}&\frac{(\text{vec } Y)'(bb'\otimes XX^+) \text{ vec } Y - 2(\text{vec } Y)'(bb'\otimes X_1X_1^+)\times \times \text{vec } Y + (\text{vec } Y)'(bb'\otimes X_1^{+\prime}X_1'X_1X_1^+) \text{ vec } Y}{b'\Omega b} \\ &= \frac{(\text{vec } Y)'(bb'\otimes XX^+) \text{ vec } Y - (\text{vec } Y)'(bb'\otimes X_1X_1^+) \text{ vec } Y}{b'\Omega b}\end{aligned} \tag{3.4.29}$$

which depends only on $b$.

Since $XX^+$ and $X_1X_1^+$ are idempotent matrices, (3.4.29) can be rewritten as:

$$\frac{[(b'\otimes XX^+) \text{ vec } Y]'[(b'\otimes XX^+) \text{ vec } Y] - [(b'\otimes X_1X_1^+) \text{ vec } Y]'[(b'\otimes X_1X_1^+) \text{ vec } Y]}{b'\Omega b} \tag{3.4.30}$$

or, since:

$$(b'\otimes XX^+) \text{ vec } Y = XX^+Yb$$

and

$$(b'\otimes X_1X_1^+) \text{ vec } Y = X_1X_1^+Yb$$

as:

$$\frac{b'(Y'XX^+Y - Y'X_1X_1^+Y)b}{b'\Omega b} \tag{3.4.31}$$

Now $(Y'XX^+Y - Y'X_1X_1^+Y)$ will be a symmetrical and $\Omega$ a symmetrical positive definite matrix. It follows[1] from the above that the minimum of (3.4.31) equals $\lambda_1$, in which $\lambda_1$ is the smallest root of the equation

$$|Y'XX^+Y - Y'X_1X_1^+Y - \lambda\Omega| = 0 \tag{3.4.32}$$

Hence this minimum is attained for each $\hat{b}$ which satisfies:

$$(Y'XX^+Y - Y'X_1X_1^+Y - \lambda_1\Omega)\hat{b} = 0 \tag{3.4.33}$$

Since:

$$\hat{c} = -(b' \otimes X_1^+) \text{ vec } Y = -X_1^+Yb$$

can be rewritten as:

$$(X_1'X_1)\hat{c} + X_1'Yb = 0$$

equations (3.4.28) and (3.4.33) can be combined:

$$\begin{pmatrix} Y'XX^+Y - \lambda_1\Omega & Y'X_1 \\ X_1'Y & X_1'X_1 \end{pmatrix} \begin{pmatrix} \hat{b} \\ \hat{c} \end{pmatrix} = 0 \tag{3.4.34}$$

Assuming, as a normalisation rule, that the first element of $\hat{b}$ is equal to $-1$, (3.4.34) will become:

$$\begin{pmatrix} Y_2'XX^+Y_2 - \lambda_1\Omega_{22} & Y_2'X_1 \\ X_1'Y_2 & X_1'X_1 \end{pmatrix} \begin{pmatrix} \bar{b}_2 \\ \bar{c} \end{pmatrix} = \begin{pmatrix} Y_2'XX^+Y_1 - \lambda_1\Omega_{21} \\ X_1'Y_1 \end{pmatrix} \tag{3.4.35}$$

in which:

- $\begin{pmatrix} \bar{b}_2 \\ \bar{c} \end{pmatrix}$ are the remaining elements of $\begin{pmatrix} \hat{b} \\ \hat{c} \end{pmatrix}$ after normalisation:
- $Y_1$ represents the first column of $Y$
- $Y_2$ represents the matrix of the remaining columns of $Y$
- $\Omega_{21}$ represents the first column of $\Omega$ minus the first element
- $\Omega_{22}$ represents the matrix of the last $m-1$ rows and the last $(m-1)$ columns of $\Omega$.

1. See C.R. Rao, *Linear Statistical Reference and its Applications*, Wiley, New York, 1965, page 59.

If $\Omega$ is known, $\lambda_1$, $\bar{b}_2$ and $\bar{c}$ can be calculated from (3.4.32) and (3.4.35).

In practice, however, $\Omega$ will generally be unknown and will then be replaced by a consistent estimator:

$$\hat{\Omega} = \frac{\hat{\eta}'\hat{\eta}}{T} \tag{3.4.36}$$

in which, in view of (3.3.9):

$$\hat{\eta} = Y - X(X'X)^{-1}X'Y \tag{3.4.37}$$

is the matrix of estimated residuals starting from the reduced form of the model (3.3.3).

Since:

$$\hat{\eta}'\hat{\eta} = Y'(I_T - XX^+)Y$$

and:

$$\left(1 + \frac{\lambda_1}{T}\right) = k$$

substitution of (3.4.36) into (3.4.32) and (3.4.35) gives:

$$|Y'Y - Y'X_1X_1^+Y - k\hat{\eta}'\hat{\eta}| = 0 \tag{3.4.38}$$

and:

$$\begin{pmatrix} Y_2'Y_2 - k\hat{\eta}_2'\hat{\eta}_2 & Y_2'X_1 \\ X_1'Y_2 & X_1'X_1 \end{pmatrix} \begin{pmatrix} \bar{b}_2 \\ \bar{c} \end{pmatrix} = \begin{pmatrix} Y_2'Y_1 - k\hat{\eta}_2'\hat{\eta}_1 \\ X_1'Y_1 \end{pmatrix} \tag{3.4.39}$$

in which: $\hat{\eta}_2'\hat{\eta}_2$ and $\hat{\eta}_2'\hat{\eta}_1$ are submatrices of $\hat{\eta}'\hat{\eta}$ corresponding to $\Omega_{22}$ and $\Omega_{21}$.

Consideration of the solution $\hat{b}_2(k)$ and $\hat{c}(k)$ of the equation system for each $k$-value gives the class of estimators known in the literature as $k$-class estimators.

## III.5 AN ASYMPTOTIC PROPERTY OF $k$-CLASS ESTIMATORS

This section will show that in certain circumstances $k$-class estimators are consistent, as follows:

Solving the estimators $\bar{b}_2$ and $\bar{c}$ from (3.4.39) gives:

$$\begin{pmatrix} \bar{b}_2 \\ \bar{c} \end{pmatrix} = \begin{pmatrix} Y_2'Y_2 - k\hat{\eta}_2'\hat{\eta}_2 & Y_2'X_1 \\ X_1'Y_2 & X_1'X_1 \end{pmatrix}^{-1} \begin{pmatrix} Y_2'Y_1 - k\hat{\eta}_2'\hat{\eta}_1 \\ X_1'Y_1 \end{pmatrix} \tag{3.5.1}$$

Taking the probability limit of (3.5.1) now gives:

$$\underset{T\to\infty}{p\lim}\begin{bmatrix}\bar{b}_2\\ \\ \bar{c}\end{bmatrix} = \underset{T\to\infty}{p\lim}\begin{bmatrix}\dfrac{Y_2' Y_2}{T} - k\dfrac{\hat{\eta}_2'\hat{\eta}_2}{T} & \dfrac{Y_2' X_1}{T}\\ \\ \dfrac{X_1' Y_2}{T} & \dfrac{X_1' X_1}{T}\end{bmatrix}^{-1} \times$$

$$\times \underset{T\to\infty}{p\lim}\begin{bmatrix}\dfrac{Y_2' Y_1}{T} - k\dfrac{\hat{\eta}_2'\hat{\eta}_1}{T}\\ \\ \dfrac{X_1' Y_1}{T}\end{bmatrix} \tag{3.5.2}$$

Since:

$$Y_2 = X\pi_{.2} + \eta_2 \tag{3.5.3}$$

$$Y_1 = Y_2 b_2 + X_1 c + \varepsilon_1 \tag{3.5.4}$$

$$\varepsilon_1 = -\eta\begin{pmatrix}-1\\ b_2\end{pmatrix} = \eta_1 - \eta_2 b_2 \tag{3.5.5}$$

in which:

$\pi_{.2}$ represents the matrix $\pi$ minus the first column, we find that:

$$-\underset{T\to\infty}{p\lim}\frac{Y_2' Y_1}{T} = \underset{T\to\infty}{p\lim}\frac{1}{T}(\pi_{.2}' X' + \eta_2')(Y_2 b_2 + X_1 c + \varepsilon_1)$$

$$= \underset{T\to\infty}{p\lim}\frac{1}{T}(\pi_{.2}' X' X\pi_{.2} b_2 + \pi_{.2}' X'\eta_2 b_2 + \eta_2' X\pi_{.2} b_2 + \eta_2'\eta_2 b_2 +$$

$$+ \pi_{.2}' X' X_1 c + \eta_2' X_1 c + \eta_2'\eta_1 - \eta_2'\eta_2 b_2)$$

$$= (\pi_{.2}' M_{xx}\pi_{.2} b_2 + \pi_{.2}' M_{xx_1} c + \Omega_{21}) \tag{3.5.6}$$

and that:

$$-\underset{T\to\infty}{p\lim}\frac{X_1' Y_1}{T} = \underset{T\to\infty}{p\lim}\frac{1}{T}X_1'(Y_2 b_2 + X_1 c + \varepsilon_1)$$

$$= \underset{T\to\infty}{p\lim}\frac{1}{T}(X_1' X\pi_{.2} b_2 + X_1'\eta_2 b_2 + X_1' X_1 c + X_1'\eta_1 - X_1'\eta_2 b_2)$$

$$= (M_{x_1 x}\pi_{.2} b_2 + M_{x_1 x_1} c) \tag{3.5.7}$$

Using these results we find for (3.5.2)

$$\underset{T\to\infty}{p\lim}\begin{bmatrix}\bar{b}_2\\ \\ \bar{c}\end{bmatrix} = \underset{T\to\infty}{p\lim}\begin{bmatrix}\dfrac{Y_2'Y_2}{T}-k\dfrac{\hat{\eta}_2'\hat{\eta}_2}{T} & \dfrac{Y_2'X_1}{T}\\ \\ \dfrac{X_1'Y_2}{T} & \dfrac{X_1'X_1}{T}\end{bmatrix}^{-1}\times$$

$$\times\left\{\begin{pmatrix}\pi_{\cdot 2}'M_{xx}\pi_{\cdot 2} & \pi_{\cdot 2}'M_{xx_1}\\ M_{x_1x}\pi_{\cdot 2} & M_{x_1x_1}\end{pmatrix}\begin{pmatrix}b_2\\ c\end{pmatrix}+\begin{pmatrix}\underset{T\to\infty}{p\lim}\,(1-k)\,\Omega_{21}\\ 0\end{pmatrix}\right\} \tag{3.5.8}$$

Now:

$$\underset{T\to\infty}{p\lim}\begin{bmatrix}\dfrac{Y_2'Y_2}{T}-k\dfrac{\hat{\eta}_2'\hat{\eta}_2}{T} & \dfrac{Y_2'X_1}{T}\\ \\ \dfrac{X_1'Y_2}{T} & \dfrac{X_1'X_1}{T}\end{bmatrix}^{-1}$$

$$=\left\{\underset{T\to\infty}{p\lim}\begin{bmatrix}\dfrac{Y_2'Y_2}{T}-k\dfrac{\hat{\eta}_2'\hat{\eta}_2}{T} & \dfrac{Y_2'X_1}{T}\\ \\ \dfrac{X_1'Y_2}{T} & \dfrac{X_1'X_1}{T}\end{bmatrix}\right\}^{-1} \tag{3.5.9}$$

provided

$$\underset{T\to\infty}{p\lim}\begin{bmatrix}\dfrac{Y_2'Y_2}{T}-k\dfrac{\hat{\eta}_2'\hat{\eta}_2}{T} & \dfrac{Y_2'X_1}{T}\\ \\ \dfrac{X_1'Y_2}{T} & \dfrac{X_1'X_1}{T}\end{bmatrix} \tag{3.5.10}$$

applies and is non-singular; see Wilks[1].

Working out (3.5.10) with the aid of (3.5.9) and:

$$\underset{T\to\infty}{p\lim}\frac{Y_2'Y_2}{T}=\underset{T\to\infty}{p\lim}\frac{1}{T}(\pi_{\cdot 2}'X'X\pi_{\cdot 2}+\pi_{\cdot 2}'X'\eta_2+\eta_2'X\pi_{\cdot 2}+\eta_2'\eta_2)$$

$$=\pi_{\cdot 2}'M_{xx}\pi_{\cdot 2}+\Omega_{22} \tag{3.5.11}$$

1. S.S. Wilks, *Mathematical Statistics*, Wiley, New York, 1963, page 103.

gives:

$$\underset{T\to\infty}{p\lim}\begin{bmatrix}\dfrac{Y_2'Y_2}{T}-k\dfrac{\hat{\eta}_2'\hat{\eta}_2}{T} & \dfrac{Y_2'X_1}{T}\\ & \\ \dfrac{X_1'Y_2}{T} & \dfrac{X_1'X_1}{T}\end{bmatrix}$$

$$=\begin{pmatrix}\pi'_{\cdot 2}M_{xx}\pi_{\cdot 2}+\underset{T\to\infty}{p\lim}\,(1-k)\,\Omega_{22} & \pi'_{\cdot 2}M_{xx_1}\\ M_{x_1x}\pi_{\cdot 2} & M_{x_1x_1}\end{pmatrix}$$

$$=\begin{pmatrix}\pi'_{\cdot 2}M_{xx}\pi_{\cdot 2} & \pi'_{\cdot 2}M_{xx_1}\\ M_{x_1x}\pi_{\cdot 2} & M_{x_1x_1}\end{pmatrix}+\underset{T\to\infty}{p\lim}\,(1-k)\begin{pmatrix}\Omega_{22} & 0\\ 0 & 0\end{pmatrix} \qquad (3.5.12)$$

The first matrix in the right-hand term of (3.5.12) can now be written:

$$\begin{pmatrix} & \pi'_{\cdot 2} & \\ I_{k_1} & & 0\end{pmatrix} M_{xx} \begin{pmatrix} \pi_{\cdot 2} & I_{k_1}\\ & 0\end{pmatrix} \qquad (3.5.13)$$

in which:

- $I_{k_1}$ represents a $k_1\times k_1$ unity matrix
- 0 represents a $k_1\times(k-k_1)$ zero matrix.

According to hypothesis 7, $M_{xx}$ has the rank $k$.

The matrix

$$\begin{pmatrix} & \pi'_{\cdot 2} & \\ I_{k_1} & & 0\end{pmatrix} \qquad (3.5.14)$$

is an $(m-1+k_1)\times k$ matrix with the rank $(m-1+k_1)$, for $m-1+k_1\leq k$. Otherwise:

$$k-k_1>m-1 \qquad (3.5.15)$$

and this is contradictory to the order condition for identification.

Furthermore, the matrix $\pi'_{22}$, consisting of the first $(m-1)$ rows and the last $(k-k_1)$ columns of $\pi'_{\cdot 2}$, has the rank $m-1$. Otherwise this would be contradictory to the rank condition for identification discussed in I.3.

It follows from the above that the first matrix of the right-hand term of (3.5.12) is non-singular.

Furthermore, $\Omega_{22}$ is non-singular; hence:

$$\begin{pmatrix} \pi'_{.2} M_{xx} \pi_{.2} + \underset{T\to\infty}{p \lim} (1-k)\Omega_{22} & \pi'_{.2} M_{xx_1} \\ M_{xx}\pi_{.2} & M_{x_1 x_1} \end{pmatrix} \tag{3.5.16}$$

will certainly not be singular if $\underset{T\to\infty}{p \lim}(1-k) \geq 0$.

Substituting (3.5.13) into (3.5.5) gives:

$$\underset{T\to\infty}{p \lim} \begin{pmatrix} \bar{b}_2 \\ \bar{c} \end{pmatrix} = \begin{pmatrix} \pi'_{.2} M_{xx} \pi_{.2} + \underset{T\to\infty}{p \lim} (1-k)\Omega_{22} & \pi'_{.2} M_{xx_1} \\ M_{x_1 x}\pi_{.2} & M_{x_1 x_1} \end{pmatrix}^{-1} \times$$

$$\times \left\{ \begin{pmatrix} \pi'_{.2} M_{xx}\pi_{.2} & \pi'_{.2} M_{xx_1} \\ M_{x_1 x}\pi_{.2} & M_{x_1 x_1} \end{pmatrix} \begin{pmatrix} b_2 \\ c \end{pmatrix} + \begin{pmatrix} \underset{T\to\infty}{p \lim} (1-k)\Omega_{21} \\ 0 \end{pmatrix} \right\} \tag{3.5.17}$$

and from (3.5.14) it can be seen immediately that $\bar{b}_2$ and $\bar{c}$ are consistent estimators only if $p \lim k$ equals 1.

The value of $p \lim k$ calculated from (3.4.38) is 1. For:

$$\underset{T\to\infty}{p \lim} \left| \frac{Y'Y}{T} - \frac{Y'X_1}{T} \left(\frac{X_1'X_1}{T}\right)^{-1} \frac{X_1'Y}{T} - k\frac{\hat{\eta}'\hat{\eta}}{T} \right|$$

$$= \left| \underset{T\to\infty}{p \lim} \left[ \frac{Y'Y}{T} - \frac{Y'X_1}{T} \left(\frac{X_1'X_1}{T}\right)^{-1} \frac{X_1'Y}{T} - k\frac{\hat{\eta}'\hat{\eta}}{T} \right] \right| = 0 \tag{3.5.18}$$

and a derivation analogous to (3.5.7) and (3.5.11) gives:

$$\underset{T\to\infty}{p \lim} \frac{Y'X_1}{T} = \pi' M_{xx_1}$$

$$\underset{T\to\infty}{p \lim} \frac{Y'Y}{T} = \pi' M_{xx}\pi + \Omega$$

so that (3.5.18) can be written:

$$|\pi'(M_{xx} - M_{xx_1} M_{x_1 x_1}^{-1} M_{x_1 x})\pi + \underset{T\to\infty}{p \lim} (1-k)\Omega| = 0 \tag{3.5.19}$$

Now:

$$M_{xx} - M_{xx_1} M_{x_1x_1}^{-1} M_{x_1x} = \begin{pmatrix} M_{x_1x_1} & M_{x_1x_2} \\ M_{x_2x_1} & M_{x_2x_2} \end{pmatrix} - \begin{pmatrix} M_{x_1x_1} & M_{x_1x_2} \\ M_{x_2x_1} & M_{x_2x_1} M_{x_1x_1}^{-1} M_{x_1x_2} \end{pmatrix} = \begin{pmatrix} 0 & 0 \\ 0 & M_{x_2x_2} - M_{x_2x_1} M_{x_1x_1}^{-1} M_{x_1x_2} \end{pmatrix} \quad (3.5.20)$$

and with the aid of (3.5.20), (3.5.19) can be written:

$$|\pi_{2.}'(M_{x_2x_2} - M_{x_2x_1} M_{x_1x_1}^{-1} M_{x_1x_2})\pi_{2.} + p \lim_{T \to \infty} (1-k)\Omega| = 0 \quad (3.5.21)$$

in which $\pi_{2.}$ represents the matrix consisting of the last $(k-k_1)$ rows of $\pi$. Matrix $\pi_{2.}$ has the rank $(m-1)$; the first matrix of (3.5.21) is thus non-negative definite and, as matrix $\Omega$ is positive-definite, $p \lim (1-k) = 0$. See Goldberger[1].

This means that the estimators calculated from (3.4.34) and (3.4.35) are consistent.

These estimators are known as the Limited Information Maximum Likelihood estimators (LIML).

Another obvious value for $k$ providing a consistent estimator is $k = 1$.

The estimators belonging to this value for $k$ are known as the two-stage least-squares estimators (2SLS).

The foregoing makes it clear that owing to this asymptotic property there is no preference as regards the above-mentioned estimation methods.

But there will be if the amount of work needed to calculate each estimator is compared; the equation system of (3.4.39) for $k = 1$ changes to:

$$\begin{pmatrix} \hat{Y}_2' \hat{Y}_2 & \hat{Y}_2' X_1 \\ X_1' Y_2 & X_1' X_1 \end{pmatrix} \begin{pmatrix} \bar{b}_2 \\ \bar{c} \end{pmatrix} = \begin{pmatrix} \hat{Y}_2' Y_1 \\ X_1' Y_1 \end{pmatrix} \quad (3.5.22)$$

or:

$$\begin{pmatrix} \bar{b}_2 \\ \bar{c} \end{pmatrix} = [(\hat{Y}_2, X_1)'(\hat{Y}_2, X_1)]^{-1} (\hat{Y}_2, X_1)' Y_1 \quad (3.5.23)$$

1. A.S. Goldberger, *Econometric Theory*, Wiley, New York, 1964, page 38.

showing that the 2SLS estimators are found by regressing $Y_1$ on $\hat{Y}_2$ and $X_1$.

Calculation of LIML estimators, however, means that (3.4.38) must be solved, which is certainly time-consuming. The 2SLS estimation method might therefore be preferred.

## III.6 MULTICOLLINEARITY WITH 2SLS AND LIML

This section is divided into two parts. Part A discusses the causes of multicollinearity for 2SLS and part B for LIML.

### *Part A*

As the preceding section has shown, the 2SLS method can be regarded as being built up as follows:

1. The best linear unbiased estimator of $\pi$, the matrix of the reduced form coefficients, is defined. With the aid of this $\hat{Y}_2$, the estimator of $Y_2$, is calculated.
2. $\hat{Y}_2$ and $X_1$ are treated as explanatory variables and $Y_1$ as the dependent variable, and the least square estimators $\bar{b}_2$ and $\bar{c}$ are calculated.

The following cases can now be described:

a. The estimated dependent variables in the equation to be estimated are multicollinear; the explanatory variables are not multicollinear.

This multicollinearity may be due to the dependent variables appearing in the equation being multicollinear, since $\hat{Y}_2$ is found by projecting the column vectors of $Y_2$ onto the space spanned by the column vectors of $X$.

As projection cannot increase the number of linear independent vectors, it follows that the rank of $\hat{Y}_2$ is less than or equal to the rank of $Y_2$.

Should the column vectors of $\hat{Y}_2$ be independent, those of $Y_2$ are also independent. The reverse does not apply however; even if the column vectors of $Y_2$ are independent, those of $\hat{Y}_2$ can certainly be dependent. For, in view of (2.3.1) and (2.3.12):

$$\hat{Y}_2 = X(X'X)^{-1}X'Y_2 \tag{3.6.1}$$

which represents a $T \times (m-1)$ matrix, whose rank is defined by that of $X'Y_2$, which may be smaller than $(m-1)$.

*Example*
Let us take the model:

$$\begin{cases} y_{1t}+b_{12}y_{2t}+b_{13}y_{3t} & = \varepsilon_{1t} \\ b_{21}y_{1t}+\quad y_{2t}+b_{23}y_{3t}+c_{21}x_{1t}+c_{22}x_{2t} & = \varepsilon_{2t}\ (t=1,2,\dots,T) \\ b_{31}y_{1t}+b_{32}y_{2t}+\quad y_{3t}+c_{31}x_{1t} & = \varepsilon_{3t} \end{cases} \qquad (3.6.2)$$

If we wish to estimate the first equation of this model, we must first determine the projections of vectors $Y_2$ and $Y_3$ on the subspace spanned by $x_1$ and $x_2$. These projections may coincide even if vectors $Y_2$ and $y_3$ do not (see fig. 3.6.3):

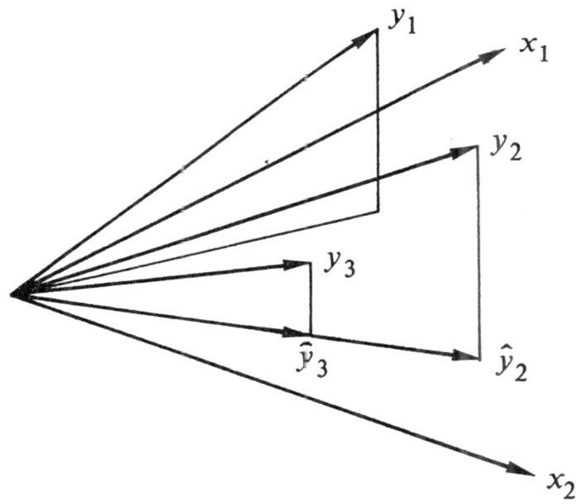


*Figure 3.6.3*

b. The explanatory variables in the equation are multicollinear; the estimated dependent variables are not.

This causes no difficulties in the first step because $Y_2$ columns can always be projected on the columns of the spanned subspace.

Difficulties emerge in the second step in expressing uniquely the projection $\hat{Y}_1$ of $Y_1$ on the columns of the subspace spanned by the matrix $(\hat{Y}_2, X_1)$, in these vectors.

Unique determination of the coefficients belonging to the $\hat{Y}_2$ column vectors will generally be possible.

c. The estimated dependent and explanatory variables in the equation are multicollinear.

This form of multicollinearity may originate in three ways. Firstly, the explanatory variables not appearing in the equation may not help to explain the dependent variables in the equation. In this event the $\hat{Y}_2$ columns will lie in the subspace spanned by the $X_1$ columns.

*Example*
Let us take the model:

$$\begin{cases} y_{1t}+b_{12}y_{2t}+c_{11}x_{1t} = \varepsilon_{1t} \\ b_{21}y_{1t}+y_{2t}+c_{21}x_{1t}+c_{22}x_{2t} = \varepsilon_{2t} \end{cases} \qquad (t=1,2,\dots,T) \qquad (3.6.4)$$

If we wish to estimate the first equation and if $x_2$ does not help to explain $y_2$, then $\hat{y}_2$ will coincide with $x_1$ (see fig. 3.6.5):

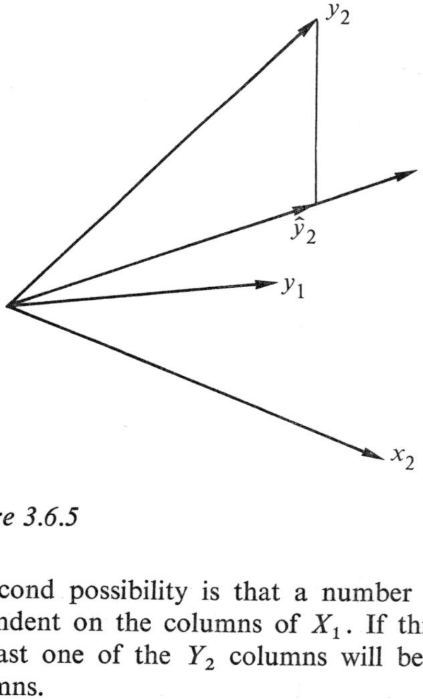


*Figure 3.6.5*

A second possibility is that a number of columns of $X_2$ are linearly dependent on the columns of $X_1$. If this number exceeds $(k_2-m+1)$, at least one of the $Y_2$ columns will be linearly dependent on the $X_1$ columns.

*Example*
For the model in the foregoing example, this situation is worked out in fig. 3.6.6.

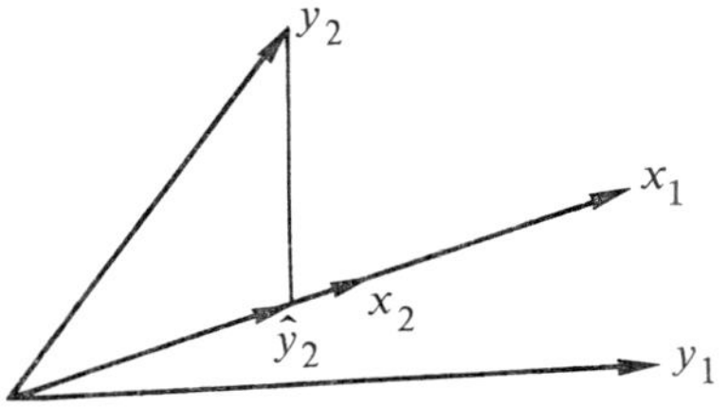


*Figure 3.6.6*

Along with this possibility, the following must be stated: Since exact multicollinearity does not occur in practice, it is possible, in spite of $x_1$ and $x_2$ being nearly multicollinear, that $x_1$ and $\hat{y}_2$ are definitely *not* multicollinear (see fig. 3.6.7).

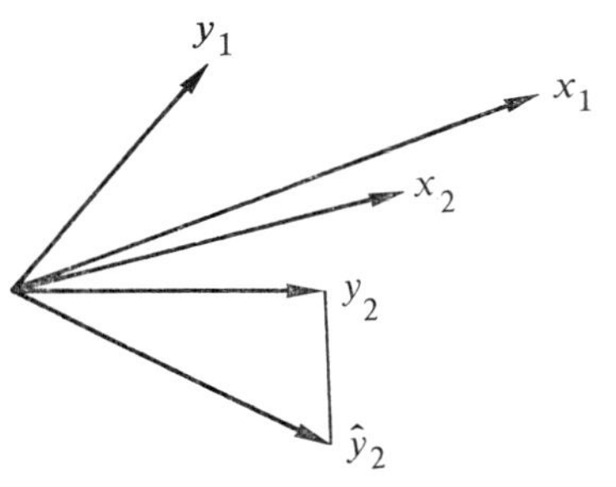


*Figure 3.6.7*

A third possibility is that the $X_2$ columns are mutually dependent. If the number of independent column-vectors of $X_2$ is less than $(m-1)$, the dimensions of the sub-space spanned by the column vectors of $X$ will be smaller than $(k_1+m-1)$, and multicollinearity will thus occur between the $\hat{Y}_2$ and $X_1$ columns.

*Example*

Let us take the model:

$$\begin{cases} y_{1t}+b_{12}y_{2t}+b_{13}y_{3t}+c_{11}x_{1t} & = \varepsilon_{1t} \\ b_{21}y_{1t}+y_{2t}+b_{23}y_{3t}+c_{21}x_{1t}+c_{22}x_{2t}+c_{23}x_{3t} & = \varepsilon_{2t} \\ b_{32}y_{2t}+y_{3t}+c_{32}x_{2t} & = \varepsilon_{3t} \end{cases}$$

$$(t=1, 2, \dots, T) \quad (3.6.8)$$

If we wish to estimate the first equation, and if $x_2$ and $x_3$ are multicollinear then $\hat{y}_2$, $\hat{y}_3$ and $x_1$ are also multicollinear (see fig. 3.6.9).

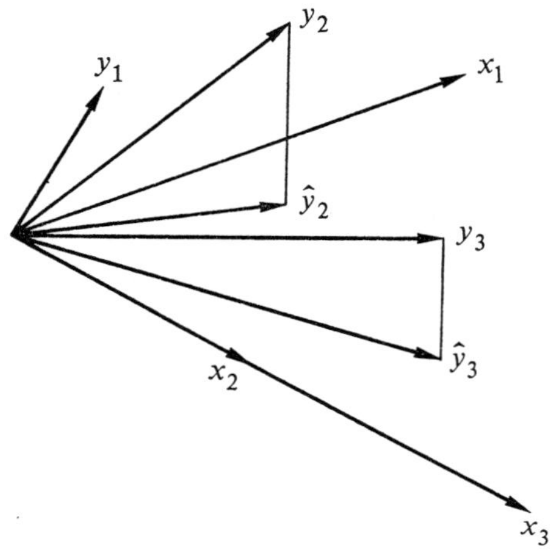


*Figure 3.6.9*

*Part B*

The LIML method derived in the last paragraph may also be regarded as a projection estimator if the derivation is slightly changed.

If the normalisation rule

$$b'\hat{\Omega}b = 1 \tag{3.6.10}$$

is applied in the second step, the following problem will be found.

Minimalise:

$$b'[Y'X(X'X)^{-1}X'Y - Y'X_1(X_1'X_1)^{-1}X_1'Y]b \tag{3.6.11}$$

allowing for (3.6.10).

A closer look at (3.6.11) shows that the matrix between the square brackets can be written:

$$[\hat{Y}\hat{Y} - \hat{\hat{Y}}'\hat{\hat{Y}}] \tag{3.6.12}$$

with:

$$\hat{\hat{Y}} = X_1(X_1'X_1)^{-1}X_1'Y \tag{3.6.13}$$

that is to say, the projections of the $Y$ column vectors on the subspace spanned by the $X_1$ column vectors.

The problem can now be rewritten:

Minimalise:

$$\left[\sum_{i=1}^{m} b_i(\hat{y}_i - \hat{\hat{y}}_i)\right]^2 \tag{3.6.14}$$

subject to the constraint (3.6.10).

$b_i$ has to be chosen – allowing for (3.6.10) – so that the vector:

$$\sum_{i=1}^{m} b_i(\hat{y}_i - \hat{\hat{y}}_i) \tag{3.6.15}$$

is of the minimum length (see fig. 3.6.16).

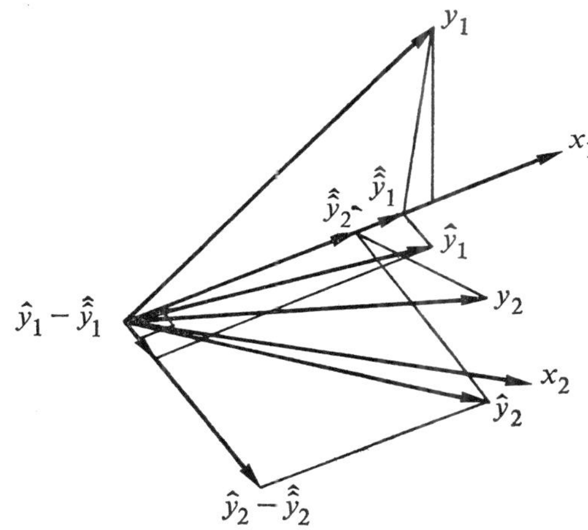


*Figure 3.6.16*

Now (3.6.15) will be the minimum in view of (3.4.32) if the characteristic vector belonging to the smallest root $\lambda$ of the equation (3.6.17) is chosen for $b$:

$$\left| Y'X(X'X)^{-1}X'Y - Y'X_1(X_1'X_1)^{-1}X_1'Y - \frac{\lambda}{T}\hat{\eta}\hat{\eta} \right| = 0 \tag{3.6.17}$$

Since:

$$(\hat{Y}-\hat{\hat{Y}})'(\hat{Y}-\hat{\hat{Y}}) = Y'[X(X'X)^{-1}X' - X_1(X_1'X_1)^{-1}X_1] \times$$
$$\times [X(X'X)^{-1}X' - X_1(X_1'X_1)^{-1}X_1']Y =$$
$$= Y'X(X'X)^{-1}X'Y - Y'X_1(X_1'X_1)^{-1}X_1'Y \qquad (3.6.18)$$

this equation can be written:

$$\left|(\hat{Y}-\hat{\hat{Y}})'(\hat{Y}-\hat{\hat{Y}}) - \frac{\lambda}{T}(Y-\hat{Y})'(Y-\hat{Y})\right| = 0 \qquad (3.6.19)$$

The following cases can now be distinguished:

a. There is a linear relationship between the variables $\hat{y}_1$ to $\hat{y}_m$. In that case there will also be a linear relationship between vectors $(\hat{y}_1 - \hat{\hat{y}}_1)$ to $(\hat{y}_m - \hat{\hat{y}}_m)$.

The matrix:

$$(\hat{Y}-\hat{\hat{Y}})'(\hat{Y}-\hat{\hat{Y}}) \qquad (3.6.20)$$

will then be singular, and the smallest root $\lambda$ of (3.6.19) will equal zero.

There is a linear combination of vectors $(\hat{y}_1 - \hat{\hat{y}}_1)$ to $(\hat{y}_m - \hat{\hat{y}}_m)$, and hence:

$$\sum_{i=1}^{m} b_i(\hat{y}_i - \hat{\hat{y}}_i) = 0 \qquad (3.6.21)$$

Applying the general normalisation rule $b_1 = -1$ will reveal two possibilities:

1. to take $(\hat{y}_1 - \hat{\hat{y}}_1)$ into the linear combination, or $b_1 \neq 0$, in which case there will be no difficulties.
2. not to take $(\hat{y}_1 - \hat{\hat{y}}_1)$ into the linear combination, in which case the minimum of (3.6.15) will equal $|\hat{y}_1 - \hat{\hat{y}}_1|^2$ and $b_2$ to $b_m$ cannot be uniquely determined.

b. If multicollinearity occurs among the column vectors of $X_1$, this will not affect determination of the coefficients $b_i$. Difficulties may occur, however, if an attempt is made to determine the coefficients belonging to the column vectors of $X_1$.

c. If the explanatory variables not appearing in the equation do not help to explain the dependent variables which do occur, then:

$$\hat{y}_i - \hat{\hat{y}}_i = 0 \qquad i = 1, 2, \ldots, m \qquad (3.6.22)$$

so that the $b_i$ will not be uniquely determined.

If a number of column vectors of $X_2$ are linearly dependent on those of $X_1$ or are mutually dependent, there will be at least two linear relations among the vectors $(\hat{y}_i - \hat{\hat{y}}_i)$ $(i = 1, 2, \ldots, m)$, if the number exceeds $k_2 - m + 1$. In this event the vectors are projected in an $(m-2)$ dimensional subspace.

The foregoing shows that the causes of multicollinearity with LIML estimators are the same as with 2SLS estimators.

But in the LIML estimation method, there is another reason for multicollinearity.

d. Even if there is no linear dependency between vectors $(\hat{y}_i - \hat{\hat{y}}_i)$ $(i = 1, 2, \ldots, m)$ it will still be possible that coefficients $b_i$ cannot be uniquely determined. Should the smallest root of (3.6.18) be multiple, there are obviously an infinite number of solutions of (3.6.11).

As regards the above it can in general be said that the LIML method is more likely to present unstable estimates than the 2SLS method.

This conclusion, combined with the fact that both estimators are consistent, whilst LIML involves considerably more arithmetic than 2SLS, is the reason why only the 2SLS method is analysed further in this chapter.

## III.7 THE GENERALISED 2SLS METHOD

The preceding section has shown how multicollinearity may appear with the 2SLS method. This section will evolve a method for dealing with these difficulties.

Firstly, multicollinearity of the error-terms – which appears in a singular covariance matrix – does not necessitate adjustment of the 2SLS method, as III.3 has shown.

Multicollinearity of dependent and explanatory variables, however, is different, and the difficulties can be solved as follows:

The projections of the column vectors of $Y_2$ on the subspace spanned by the column vectors of $X$ are determined with the best linear *P*-unbiased estimators of $\pi$ as derived in III.3.

These projections equal:

$$\hat{Y}_2 = X(X'X)^{+}X'Y_2 \tag{3.7.1}$$

The second step consists of regression of $Y_1$ on $Y_2$ and $X_1$. Just as in the preceding paragraph, it will be possible for one or more linear relations to exist between the column vectors of the matrix $(\hat{Y}_2, X_1)$.

In that event it will not be possible to determine best linear unbiased estimators of $b_2$ and $c$, but best linear $P$-unbiased estimators can certainly be determined.

In pursuance of (2.5.22), therefore:

$$\begin{pmatrix} \bar{b}_2 \\ \\ \bar{c} \end{pmatrix} = [(\hat{Y}_2, X_1)'(\hat{Y}_2, X_1)]^+ (\hat{Y}_2, X_1)' Y_1 \tag{3.7.2}$$

The asymptotic properties of these estimators will be reviewed in this section. For this purpose, however, hypotheses 3 and 7 in III.2 must be adjusted, and from now on they will be replaced by:

*Hypothesis 3a*

The $T \times k$ matrix $X$ of observations of the $k$ explanatory variables has the rank $r < k$ for each $T$.

*Hypothesis 7a*

$$\lim_{T \to \infty} = \frac{1}{T}(X'X) \text{ exists and has the rank } r.$$

Roughly speaking, the latter hypothesis implies that the number and composition of linear relations between $X$-columns remain unchanged if $T \to \infty$.

It follows from hypotheses 3a and 7a that

$$\lim_{T \to \infty} \left(\frac{X'X}{T}\right)^+ = \left(\lim_{T \to \infty} \frac{X'X}{T}\right)^+ \tag{3.7.3}$$

Furthermore, the following hypotheses apply for obvious reasons:

*Hypothesis 3b*

The $T \times (m + k_1 - 1)$ matrix $(\hat{Y}_2, X_1)$ has the rank $s \leqq (mk_1 - 1)$ for each $T$.

*Hypothesis 7b*

$$\lim \frac{1}{T}(\hat{Y}_2, X_1)(\hat{Y}_2, X_1) \text{ exists and has the rank } s.$$

If all the hypotheses are satisfied the following asymptotic property can be proved:

$$\underset{T\to\infty}{p\lim}\begin{pmatrix}\bar{b}_2\\ \bar{c}\end{pmatrix}=\underset{T\to\infty}{p\lim}\begin{pmatrix}\hat{Y}_2'\hat{Y}_2 & \hat{Y}_2'X_1\\ X_1'\hat{Y}_2 & X_1'X_1\end{pmatrix}^{+}\begin{pmatrix}Y_2'Y_1\\ X_1'Y_1\end{pmatrix} \tag{3.7.4}$$

Since:

$$\hat{Y}_2 = X(X'X)^{+}X'Y_2 \tag{3.7.5}$$

we find for (3.7.4):

$$\underset{T\to\infty}{p\lim}\begin{pmatrix}\bar{b}_2\\ \bar{c}\end{pmatrix}=\underset{T\to\infty}{p\lim}\begin{pmatrix}Y_2'X(X'X)^{+}X'Y_2 & Y_2'X(X'X)^{+}X'X_1\\ X_1'X(X'X)^{+}X'Y_2 & X_1'X_1\end{pmatrix}^{+}\times$$
$$\times\begin{pmatrix}Y_2'X(X'X)^{+}X'Y_1\\ X_1'X(X'X)^{+}X'Y_1\end{pmatrix} \tag{3.7.6}$$

$$=\underset{T\to\infty}{p\lim}\begin{bmatrix}\frac{Y_2'X}{T}\left(\frac{X'X}{T}\right)^{+}\frac{X'Y_2}{T} & \frac{Y_2'X}{T}\left(\frac{X'X}{T}\right)^{+}\frac{X'X_1}{T}\\ \frac{X_1'X}{T}\left(\frac{X'X}{T}\right)^{+}\frac{X'Y_2}{T} & \frac{X_1'X_1}{T}\end{bmatrix}^{+}\times$$

$$\times\begin{bmatrix}\frac{Y_2'X}{T}\left(\frac{X'X}{T}\right)^{+}\frac{X'Y_1}{T}\\ \frac{X_1'X}{T}\left(\frac{X'X}{T}\right)^{+}\frac{X'Y_1}{T}\end{bmatrix}$$

With the aid of derivations analogous to (3.5.4) and (3.5.8) we find:

$$\underset{T\to\infty}{p\lim}\frac{X'Y_2}{T}=M_{xx}\pi_{\cdot 2}$$

and:

$$\underset{T\to\infty}{p\lim}\frac{X'Y_1}{T}=M_{xx}\pi_{\cdot 2}b_2+M_{xx_1}c$$

Taking into account (3.7.3), substitution of these results into (3.7.7) gives:

$$\underset{T\to\infty}{p \lim} \begin{bmatrix} \frac{Y_2'X}{T}\left(\frac{X'X}{T}\right)^+ \frac{X'Y_2}{T} & \frac{Y_2'X}{T}\left(\frac{X'X}{T}\right)^+ \frac{X'X_1}{T} \\ \frac{X_1'X}{T}\left(\frac{X'X}{T}\right)^+ \frac{X'Y_2}{T} & \frac{X_1'X_1}{T} \end{bmatrix}^+ \times$$

$$\times \begin{pmatrix} \pi_{\cdot 2}' M_{xx} M_{xx}^+ M_{xx} \pi_{\cdot 2} & \pi_{\cdot 2}' M_{xx} M_{xx}^+ M_{xx_1} \\ M_{x_1 x} M_{xx}^+ M_{xx} \pi_{\cdot 2} & M_{x_1 x} M_{xx}^+ M_{xx_1} \end{pmatrix} \begin{pmatrix} b_2 \\ c \end{pmatrix} \qquad (3.7.7)$$

Taking into account hypotheses 3b and 7b and that:

$$M_{xx} M_{xx}^+ M_{xx_1} = M_{xx_1}$$

and:

$$M_{x_1 x} M_{xx}^+ M_{xx_1} = M_{x_1 x_1}$$

we find for (3.7.7):

$$\underset{T\to\infty}{p \lim} \begin{pmatrix} \bar{b}_2 \\ \bar{c} \end{pmatrix} = \begin{pmatrix} \pi_{\cdot 2}' M_{xx} \pi_{\cdot 2} & \pi_{\cdot 2}' M_{xx_1} \\ M_{x_1 x} \pi_{\cdot 2} & M_{x_1 x_1} \end{pmatrix}^+ \begin{pmatrix} \pi_{\cdot 2}' M_{xx} \pi_{\cdot 2} & \pi_{\cdot 2}' M_{xx_1} \\ M_{x_1 x} \pi_{\cdot 2} & M_{x_1 x_1} \end{pmatrix} \begin{pmatrix} b_2 \\ c \end{pmatrix} \qquad (3.7.8)$$

That is to say, $\bar{b}_2$ and $\bar{c}$ are estimators with the asymptotic minimum bias.

If the vector $\begin{pmatrix} b_2 \\ c \end{pmatrix}$ belongs to the subspace spanned by the columns of $(\hat{Y}_2, X_1)'$ the estimator is even consistent.

The next chapter will try to find some small sample properties of this generalised 2SLS with the aid of a simulation study.

# IV. A Monte-Carlo study

## IV.1 INTRODUCTION

The theory of the estimation methods discussed in Chapter II actually involves no difficulties at all. In fact, the matrix of observations of the explanatory variables $X$ is of full rank and in such a case the least squares method is applied; though if matrix $X$ is not of full rank it may be better to use the best linear $P$-unbiased estimators.

The same principle applies to the estimation methods discussed in Chapter III. If matrices $X$ and $(\hat{Y}_2, X_1)$ are of full rank, then two-stage least squares are applied; if, however, one or both of the matrices are not of full rank, it is advisable to use the best linear $P$-unbiased estimators.

As already observed in I.4: matters are different in practice. Matrix $X$ will practically always be of full rank but often ill-conditioned, i.e. det. $(X'X) \approx 0$, as one or more linear relations exist between the various variables. The variances of the least squares estimators of the coefficients belonging to variables between which the linear connections exist, will generally be great. The theory of Chapters II and III may solve this difficulty.

In approximating matrix $X$ with $\bar{X}$, which is not of full rank, the linear $P$-unbiased estimators can be continued with. The question arises whether this approximation of $X$ with $\bar{X}$ does not in fact introduce greater incorrectness in the estimate than working with the ill-conditioned matrix $X$.

The Monte-Carlo study in this Chapter is a pilot study for arriving at a tentative conclusion. It is therefore limited to a small model involving some factors only – viz. those having the greatest influence on multicollinearity.

These factors are taken from the recent Monte-Carlo studies by Summers [1965], Quandt [1965], Cragg [1967], Seibt [1968] and Mosbaek and Wold [1970], which are discussed in §2. The model discussed in the present study and generation of the data are given in §3, whilst the results are analysed in §4.

It should be pointed out that it is impossible to generalise these results as such to larger models.

## IV.2 SOME RECENT MONTE-CARLO STUDIES

This section discusses some recent Monte-Carlo studies. We shall confine ourselves to the parts dealing with multicollinearity effects on the limited information maximum likelihood (LIML) and the two-stage least squares (2SLS) method.

Other factors strengthening or blurring multicollinearity effects will also be taken into account.

The notation of the various studies has been adapted to that used in this volume.

### 1. *Summers' study*

The model which Summers started with was:

$$\begin{bmatrix} 1 & b_{12} \\ 1 & b_{22} \end{bmatrix} \begin{bmatrix} y_{1t} \\ y_{2t} \end{bmatrix} + \begin{bmatrix} c_{10} & c_{11} & c_{12} & 0 & 0 \\ c_{20} & 0 & 0 & c_{23} & c_{24} \end{bmatrix} \begin{bmatrix} x_{0t} \\ x_{1t} \\ x_{2t} \\ x_{3t} \\ x_{4t} \end{bmatrix} = \begin{bmatrix} \varepsilon_{1t} \\ \varepsilon_{2t} \end{bmatrix}$$

$$t = 1, 2, \ldots, T \qquad (4.2.1)$$

in which: $y_1$ and $y_2$ represent endogenous variables
$x_0$ to $x_4$ represent exogenous variables
$\varepsilon_1$ and $\varepsilon_2$ represent error-terms.

The values of the exogenous variables were fixed for the different replications. In order to determine the multicollinearity effect, however, two sets of data of the exogenous variables were used. For the first set they were $x_1$ to $x_4$, which were weakly correlated (set $\alpha$), for the other they were $x_1$ to $x_4$, which were strongly correlated (set $\beta$).

The error-terms were drawn from a binormal distribution with zero expectation and covariance matrix $\Sigma$.

The values of the endogenous variables were calculated for each draw with the aid of the reduced model form. The reduced form was found by starting from combinations of matrices $B_1$, $B_2$, $B_3$ and $C$. Matrices $B_1$, $B_2$ and $B_3$ differed only in the value of the $b_{12}$-coefficient, which was lowest for $B_1$ and highest for $B_3$.

The following experiments were carried out:

I. 50 samples of 20 observations of error-terms were simulated. The accompanying values of the endogenous variables were calculated with matrices $B_1$, $C$ and the data set $\alpha$ of the exogenous variables.

II. as in I but with data set $\beta$ of the exogenous variables.

III. as in I but with matrix $B_2$ replacing $B_1$.

IV. as in III but with data set $\beta$ of the exogenous variables.

V. as in I but with matrix $B_3$ replacing $B_1$.

VI. as in V but with data set $\beta$ of the exogenous variables.

VII. 50 samples of 40 observations of the error-terms were simulated. The accompanying values of the endogenous variables were calculated with matrices $B_2$, $C$ and the data set $\alpha$ of the exogenous variables.

VIII. as in VII but with data set $\beta$ of the exogenous variables.

From the results of experiments I to VIII, Summers calculated estimators for the structural parameters with LIML and 2SLS.

For each estimation method, Summers calculated the root of the mean-square error (RMSE)[1] and used it as a measure of ranking both estimation methods. The RMSE's for LIML and 2 SLS are shown in table (4.2.2).

From the results in this table, Summers reaches the following conclusions:

a. Comparison of experiments with data set $\alpha$ and with data set $\beta$ shows that multicollinearity in the exogenous variables has markedly

1. The RMSE represents:

$$\frac{\sum_{i=1}^{n}(t_i-\theta)^2}{n} = \frac{\sum_{i=1}^{n}(t_i-t_m)^2}{n} + \frac{\sum_{i=1}^{n}(t_m-\theta)^2}{n} = \text{VARIANCE}+\text{BIAS}^2$$

in which: $\theta$ represents the parameter to be estimated
$t_i$ represents the estimator from the 1st sample
$t_m$ represents the average of the $n$ estimators.

more effect on the accuracy of LIML estimators than on that of 2SLS estimators (with a sample size of 20). Summers' figures (not given here) show that the increase in the RMSE is largely attributable to the increase in variance. These results confirm Klein and Nakamura's [1962] qualitative directed analysis.

*Table 4.2.2* RMSE'*s of the structural coefficients*

| *Experiment No.* | *Method* | $b_{12}$ | $c_{11}$ | $c_{12}$ | $c_{10}$ | $b_{22}$ | $c_{23}$ | $c_{24}$ | $c_{20}$ |
|---|---|---|---|---|---|---|---|---|---|
| I | LIML | 0.046 | 0.208 | 0.112 | 21.2 | 0.053 | 0.605 | 0.056 | 69.3 |
| | 2SLS | 0.046 | 0.208 | 0.112 | 21.2 | 0.051 | 0.603 | 0.054 | 69.1 |
| II | LIML | 0.750 | 3.74 | 0.738 | 260. | 0.076 | 1.25 | 0.100 | 138. |
| | 2SLS | 0.228 | 1.10 | 0.290 | 83.7 | 0.067 | 1.21 | 0.091 | 133. |
| III | LIML | 0.089 | 0.180 | 0.105 | 22.5 | 0.107 | 0.638 | 0.054 | 74.4 |
| | 2SLS | 0.091 | 0.181 | 0.105 | 22.4 | 0.109 | 0.638 | 0.053 | 74.6 |
| IV | LIML | 0.697 | 1.60 | 0.405 | 124. | 0.163 | 1.27 | 0.104 | 139. |
| | 2SLS | 0.434 | 1.23 | 0.264 | 75.6 | 0.154 | 1.21 | 0.095 | 131. |
| V | LIML | 0.132 | 0.173 | 0.105 | 22.3 | 0.182 | 0.669 | 0.062 | 75.0 |
| | 2SLS | 0.133 | 0.173 | 0.105 | 22.3 | 0.175 | 0.668 | 0.061 | 75.1 |
| VI | LIML | 1.75 | 2.60 | 0.714 | 208. | 0.268 | 1.29 | 0.108 | 141. |
| | 2SLS | 0.875 | 1.29 | 0.311 | 103. | 0.242 | 1.27 | 0.102 | 139. |
| VII | LIML | 0.070 | 0.140 | 0.076 | 15.0 | 0.084 | 0.407 | 0.037 | 49.4 |
| | 2SLS | 0.069 | 0.140 | 0.076 | 15.0 | 0.084 | 0.406 | 0.037 | 49.3 |
| VIII | LIML | 0.344 | 0.841 | 0.214 | 71.1 | 0.110 | 0.855 | 0.071 | 92.2 |
| | 2SLS | 0.334 | 0.822 | 0.210 | 70.0 | 0.111 | 0.853 | 0.072 | 92.0 |

b. Comparison of experiments I, III, and V, and II, IV and VI respectively shows that an increase in the non-diagonal element $b_{12}$ gives rise to a slight increase in the RMSE. This might suggest that an increase in interdependency in the model affects the exactness of the estimation methods.
This will be reverted to later.

c. Comparison of experiments VII and VIII shows that even with a sample size of 40 multicollinearity has obviously more influence on the exactness of the LIML estimators than on that of the 2SLS estimators.

## 2. *Quandt's study*

The model which Quandt used was:

$$\begin{bmatrix} 1 & b_{12} & b_{13} & b_{14} \\ b_{21} & 1 & b_{23} & b_{24} \\ b_{31} & b_{32} & 1 & b_{34} \\ b_{41} & b_{42} & b_{43} & 1 \end{bmatrix} \begin{bmatrix} y_{1t} \\ y_{2t} \\ y_{3t} \\ y_{4t} \end{bmatrix} +$$

$$+ \begin{bmatrix} c_{11} & c_{12} & c_{13} & 0 & 0 & 0 & 0 \\ 0 & c_{22} & 0 & 0 & c_{25} & 0 & c_{27} \\ 0 & 0 & c_{33} & c_{34} & c_{35} & 0 & 0 \\ 0 & 0 & c_{43} & 0 & c_{45} & c_{46} & 0 \end{bmatrix} \begin{bmatrix} x_{1t} \\ x_{2t} \\ x_{3t} \\ x_{4t} \\ x_{5t} \\ x_{6t} \\ x_{7t} \end{bmatrix} = \begin{bmatrix} \varepsilon_{1t} \\ \varepsilon_{2t} \\ \varepsilon_{3t} \\ \varepsilon_{4t} \end{bmatrix} \qquad (4.2.3)$$

$t = 1, 2, \dots T$

in which: $y_1$ to $y_4$ are endogenous variables
$x_1$ to $x_7$ are exogenous variables
$\varepsilon_1$ to $\varepsilon_4$ are error-terms.

The values of the exogenous variables were fixed for the various replications. In order to determine the effect of multicollinearity, however, only two data sets of exogenous variables were used. For one data set $x_1$ to $x_7$ were weakly to moderately correlated (set $\alpha$); for the other set $x_1$ to $x_7$ were strongly correlated (set $\beta$).

The error-terms were taken from a multinormal distribution with zero expectation and covariance matrix $\Sigma_1$ or $\Sigma_2$.

Matrix $\Sigma_2$ was a unit matrix; the non-diagonal elements of matrix $\Sigma_1$ differed from zero.

The endogenous-variable values were calculated for each draw with the reduced model form, found by starting from combinations of matrices $B_1$, $B_2$, $B_3$, $B_4$ and $B_5$, and $C_1$ and $C_2$.

Nine non-diagonal elements of matrix $B_1$ equal 0; six non-diagonal elements of matrices $B_2$, $B_3$, $B_4$ equal 0. Three non-diagonal elements of matrix $B_5$ equal 0.

Matrices $C_1$ and $C_2$ differ only in the value of coefficient $c_{27}$. For $C_1$ this is 0 and for $C_2 \neq 0$.

The following experiments were next carried out:

I. 100 samples of 20 observations of error-terms with covariance matrix $\Sigma_1$ were simulated. The endogenous-variable values for each combination of matrices $B_i$, $C_j$ ($i = 1, 2, \dots 5$; $j = 1, 2$), and the data sets $\alpha$ and $\beta$ of exogenous variables were calculated.
These combinations were numbered as shown in table 4.2.4.

II. 100 samples of 20 observations of the error-terms with covariance matrix $\Sigma_2$ were simulated. The accompanying endogenous-variable values were calculated for each combination of matrices $B_1$, $C_j$ ($j = 1, 2$), and for the data sets $\alpha$ and $\beta$ of the exogenous variables. These combinations were numbered as shown in table 4.2.4.

*Table 4.2.4 Numbers of various combinations*

| | | | | $\Sigma_1$ | | | $\Sigma_2$ |
|---|---|---|---|---|---|---|---|
| | | $B_1$ | $B_2$ | $B_3$ | $B_4$ | $B_5$ | $B_1$ |
| $\alpha$ | $C_1$ | 1 | 2 | 3 | 4 | 5 | 6 |
| | $C_2$ | 7 | 8 | 9 | 10 | 11 | 12 |
| $\beta$ | $C_1$ | 13 | 14 | 15 | 16 | 17 | 18 |
| | $C_2$ | 19 | 20 | 21 | 22 | 23 | 24 |

Proceeding from the results of experiments I and II, Quandt calculated the estimators of the structural parameters of the equation with 2SLS.

For each of these coefficients, he calculated different criteria for the 'performance' of the 2SLS estimators including the RMSE. His study does not, however, state the values of these criteria.

But the following conclusions are given:

a. Comparison of $\alpha$ and $\beta$ experiments shows that multicollinearity has a marked influence on the exactness of the 2SLS estimators.
b. Comparison of experiments 1 to 5, 7 to 11, 13 to 17, 19 to 23 shows that an increase in the number of zeros among the non-diagonal elements of a matrix makes the 2SLS estimators more exact.
c. Comparison of experiments with the $C_1$ and $C_2$ matrices shows that over-identification results in more exact estimators (this will happen with the $C_2$ matrix) than exact identification (this will happen with the $C_1$ matrix).
d. Comparison of experiments 1, 7, 13 and 19 with 6, 12, 18 and 24

leads to no definite conclusion regarding the effect of the number of zeros in the covariance matrix of the error-terms on the 2SLS estimation method.

3. *Cragg's study*

Cragg started from the following model:

$$\begin{bmatrix} 1 & b_{12} & b_{13} \\ b_{21} & 1 & 0 \\ 0 & b_{32} & 1 \end{bmatrix} \begin{bmatrix} y_{1t} \\ y_{2t} \\ y_{3t} \end{bmatrix} + \begin{bmatrix} c_{11} & c_{12} & 0 & 0 & c_{15} & 0 & 0 \\ c_{21} & 0 & c_{23} & 0 & c_{25} & 0 & c_{27} \\ c_{31} & 0 & c_{33} & c_{34} & 0 & c_{36} & 0 \end{bmatrix} \begin{bmatrix} x_{1t} \\ x_{2t} \\ x_{3t} \\ x_{4t} \\ x_{5t} \\ x_{6t} \\ x_{7t} \end{bmatrix} = \begin{bmatrix} \varepsilon_{1t} \\ \varepsilon_{2t} \\ \varepsilon_{3t} \end{bmatrix} \quad (4.2.5)$$

$t = 1, 2, \ldots T$

in which: $y_1$ to $y_3$ represent endogenous variables
$x_1$ to $x_7$ represent exogenous variables
$\varepsilon_1$ to $\varepsilon_3$ represent error-terms.

The following can be quoted from the part of Cragg's study of interest for present purposes:

The values of the exogenous variables were fixed over the various replications. They were generated by random sampling from uniform distribution with the range 0-100.

In order to study the influence of multicollinearity, six different linear combinations of these data sets $\alpha$ were used, chosen in such a way that data sets ($\alpha_1$ to $\alpha_6$) calculated from these combinations were correlated to an increasing extent.

The error-terms were drawn from a multinormal distribution with zero expectation and covariance matrix $\Sigma$. For each draw, the values of the endogenous variables were calculated with the reduced model form found from the given matrices $B$ and $C$.

The following experiments were now carried out:

I. 50 samples of 20 observations of the error-terms were simulated. The accompanying values of the endogenous variables were calculated for the various data sets $\alpha$, $\alpha_1$ to $\alpha_6$ of the exogenous variables.

From the results of these experiments Cragg calculated estimators for the structural parameters of the model with LIML and 2SLS. Comparison of these estimators led to the following conclusions:

a. Comparison of the experiments with data sets $\alpha$, $\alpha_1$ to $\alpha_6$ confirms the conclusions of both previous studies: namely that multicollinearity has a marked influence on the exactness of LIML and also on the 2SLS estimators. It should, however, be observed that though correlations between the exogenous variables were higher for a higher index of the data sets, the increase in this index is not always accompanied by an increase in the deviations of the estimators from the real values of the coefficient.
b. Comparison of LIML and 2SLS estimators does not indicate that either method is preferable to the other.

4. *Seibt's study*

Seibt started from the following model:

$$\begin{pmatrix} 1 & b_{12} \\ b_{21} & 1 \end{pmatrix} \begin{pmatrix} y_{1t} \\ y_{2t} \end{pmatrix} + \begin{pmatrix} c_{11} & c_{12} & c_{13} & 0 & 0 \\ c_{21} & 0 & 0 & c_{24} & c_{25} \end{pmatrix} \begin{bmatrix} x_{1t} \\ x_{2t} \\ x_{3t} \\ x_{4t} \\ x_{5t} \end{bmatrix} = \begin{pmatrix} \varepsilon_{1t} \\ \varepsilon_{2t} \end{pmatrix} \qquad (4.2.6)$$

$t = 1, 2, \ldots T$

in which: $y_1$ and $y_2$ are endogenous variables
$x_1$ to $x_5$ are exogenous variables
$\varepsilon_1$ and $\varepsilon_2$ are error-terms.

The part of Seibt's study of interest for present purposes is:

The values of the exogenous variables were fixed for the various replications. They were generated by random sampling from a uniform distribution with the range (0-100) (data set $\alpha$).

In order to check the influence of multicollinearity, it was introduced by adding a trend to each variable. Owing to this, data sets $\alpha_1$ to $\alpha_3$ were found, which were numbered in order of increasing multicollinearity due to an increasing trend, and data sets $\alpha_4$ to $\alpha_6$, which were also numbered in order of increasing multicollinearity but now due to a decreasing trend.

The error-terms of the reduced form were drawn at random from a binormal distribution with zero expectation and as the covariance matrix a diagonal matrix $\Omega$.

The values of the endogenous variables were calculated with the reduced model form found from the given matrices $B$ and $C$.

The following experiments were carried out:

I. 7 times 50 samples of 15 observations of the error-terms were simulated. Each of these sample-sets was combined with one of the data sets $\alpha$, $\alpha_1$ to $\alpha_6$ of the exogenous variables.
The endogenous variables going with the above were calculated with the matrix $(B, C)$.

From the results of these experiments Seibt calculated the estimators of the structural parameters of the equation of the model, with the LIML and 2SLS methods. For both estimation methods, Seibt calculated the RMSE's for each coefficient; these are shown in table 4.2.7.

From the results shown in this table, Seibt arrived at the following conclusions:

Comparison of the experiments with the various data sets shows that multicollinearity influences the exactness of both estimation methods

*Table 4.2.7* RMSE *of structural coefficients*

| *Data sets* | *Method* | $b_{12}$ | $c_{11}$ | $c_{12}$ | $c_{13}$ | $b_{21}$ | $c_{21}$ | $c_{24}$ | $c_{25}$ |
|---|---|---|---|---|---|---|---|---|---|
| $\alpha$ | LIML | 0.544 | 7.855 | 0.664 | 0.436 | 0.062 | 21.56 | 0.094 | 0.070 |
| | 2SLS | 0.558 | 7.997 | 0.697 | 0.450 | 0.062 | 21.48 | 0.093 | 0.070 |
| $\alpha_1$ | LIML | 0.928 | 9.691 | 1.158 | 0.716 | 0.069 | 21.90 | 0.115 | 0.109 |
| | 2SLS | 0.904 | 9.605 | 1.123 | 0.702 | 0.067 | 21.39 | 0.114 | 0.108 |
| $\alpha_2$ | LIML | 1.141 | 9.104 | 1.439 | 0.860 | 0.074 | 23.32 | 0.178 | 0.174 |
| | 2SLS | 1.072 | 9.011 | 1.348 | 0.812 | 0.072 | 22.59 | 0.176 | 0.171 |
| $\alpha_3$ | LIML | 1.249 | 8.743 | 1.590 | 0.927 | 0.077 | 24.22 | 0.305 | 0.288 |
| | 2SLS | 1.141 | 8.607 | 1.452 | 0.850 | 0.075 | 23.39 | 0.301 | 0.284 |
| $\alpha_4$ | LIML | 0.652 | 6.960 | 0.841 | 0.562 | 0.098 | 43.37 | 0.147 | 0.068 |
| | 2SLS | 0.671 | 7.260 | 0.851 | 0.585 | 0.096 | 41.98 | 0.145 | 0.067 |
| $\alpha_5$ | LIML | 0.945 | 10.21 | 1.597 | 1.091 | 0.172 | 76.55 | 0.260 | 0.093 |
| | 2SLS | 0.974 | 10.70 | 1.558 | 1.133 | 0.155 | 69.08 | 0.238 | 0.090 |
| $\alpha_6$ | LIML | 1.103 | 11.78 | 2.360 | 1.573 | 0.210 | 93.48 | 0.323 | 0.108 |
| | 2SLS | 1.127 | 12.32 | 2.248 | 1.616 | 0.182 | 80.86 | 0.285 | 0.104 |

and this influence is perhaps somewhat greater with LIML than with 2SLS estimators.

### 5. *Mosbaek and Wold's study*

The models from which Mosbaek and Wold started included the following:

$$\begin{pmatrix} 1 & b_{12} \\ b_{21} & 1 \end{pmatrix} \begin{pmatrix} y_{1t} \\ y_{2t} \end{pmatrix} + \begin{pmatrix} c_{11} & c_{12} & 0 & 0 \\ 0 & 0 & c_{23} & c_{24} \end{pmatrix} \begin{bmatrix} x_{1t} \\ x_{2t} \\ x_{3t} \\ x_{4t} \end{bmatrix} = \begin{pmatrix} \varepsilon_{1t} \\ \varepsilon_{2t} \end{pmatrix} \qquad (4.2.8)$$

$t = 1, 2, \ldots T$

in which: $y_1$ and $y_2$ are endogenous variables
$x_1$ to $x_4$ are exogenous variables
$\varepsilon_1$ and $\varepsilon_2$ are error-terms.

and

$$\begin{bmatrix} 1 & b_{12} & b_{13} \\ b_{21} & 1 & b_{23} \\ b_{31} & b_{32} & 1 \end{bmatrix} \begin{bmatrix} y_{1t} \\ y_{2t} \\ y_{3t} \end{bmatrix} + \begin{bmatrix} c_{11} & c_{12} & 0 & 0 & 0 & 0 \\ 0 & 0 & c_{23} & c_{24} & 0 & 0 \\ 0 & 0 & 0 & 0 & c_{25} & c_{26} \end{bmatrix} \begin{bmatrix} x_{1t} \\ x_{2t} \\ x_{3t} \\ x_{4t} \\ x_{5t} \\ x_{6t} \end{bmatrix} = \begin{bmatrix} \varepsilon_{1t} \\ \varepsilon_{2t} \\ \varepsilon_{3t} \end{bmatrix} \qquad (4.2.9)$$

$t = 1, 2, \ldots T$

in which: $y_1$ to $y_3$ are endogenous variables
$x_1$ to $x_6$ are exogenous variables
$\varepsilon_1$ to $\varepsilon_3$ are error-terms.

The values of the exogenous variables were drawn for each replication from a multinormal distribution with zero expectation and a covariance matrix which is either a unit matrix or – in order to study the multicollinearity effect – two non-diagonal matrices.

The error-terms of the reduced form are drawn from a multinormal distribution with zero expectation and diagonal matrices $\Omega_1$ for the first model and $\Omega_2$ for the second model. The values of the endogenous variables were calculated for each draw with the aid of the reduced form of the model found for the first model from matrices $(B_i C_i)$ $(i = 1, 2, \dots 7)$ and for the second model from matrices $(B_i C_i)$ $(i = 8, 9, \dots 13)$.

The following experiments were now carried out:

I. $5 \times 100$ samples of 40 observations of the error-terms and $5 \times 100$ samples of 40 observations of the independent exogenous variables were simulated.
Each of these samples was combined with the matrices $(B_i C_i)$ $(i=1, 2, \dots 5)$.
The matrices $B_1$, $B_2$ and $B_3$ were anti-symmetrical matrices with increasing non-diagonal elements in this order. Matrices $B_4$ and $B_5$ were asymmetrical matrices with increasing non-diagonal elements in this order. Matrices $C_i$ belonging to matrices $B_i$ were chosen so that $c_{11} = c_{12}$, $c_{23} = c_{24}$ and $V(y_i) = 1$ $(i = 1, 2)$.

II. $2 \times 100$ samples of 40 observations of correlated exogenous variables were simulated.
One set of 100 samples, viz. those in which the variables $x_1$ and $x_2$ and the variables $x_3$ and $x_4$ were positively correlated, were combined with matrices $(B_6, C_6)$.
The other set of 100 samples, in which the variables $x_1$ and $x_2$ and the variables $x_3$ and $x_4$ were negatively correlated, were combined with matrices $(B_7, C_7)$.
Matrices $B_6$ and $B_7$ equalled $B_2$; matrices $C_6$ and $C_7$ were chosen in such a way that:

$$c_{11} = c_{12},\ c_{23} = c_{24} \text{ and } V(y_i) = 1\ (i = 1, 2).$$

III. $6 \times 100$ samples of 40 observations of the error-terms and $6 \times 100$ samples of 40 observations of the independent exogenous variables were simulated.
Each of these samples was combined with one of the matrices $(B_i, C_i)$ $(i = 8, 9, \dots 13)$.
Matrices $B_8$, $B_9$ and $B_{10}$ contained 3 non-diagonal elements unequal to zero. These non-diagonal elements increased in the order $B_8$, $B_9$, $B_{10}$.
Matrices $B_{11}$, $B_{12}$ and $B_{13}$ contained no zeros, and the non-diagonal elements of the matrix increased in the order $B_{11}$, $B_{12}$, whilst the elements of $B_{12}$ and $B_{13}$ differed only in sign.

From the results of these experiments, Mosbaek and Wold calculated the estimator of the structural parameters of the model with the 2 SLS method.

The RMSE's were calculated and are listed in tables 4.2.10 and 4.2.11; Mosbaek and Wold arrived at the following conclusions:

a. Experiments I $B_1$, $B_2$ and $B_3$ show that the increase in the non-diagonal elements is linked up with an increase in the RMSE of all coefficients.
   But it follows from experiments I $B_4$ and $B_5$ that the ratio between coefficients $b_{12}$ and $b_{21}$ greatly influences the magnitude of the RMSE.

*Table 4.2.10* RMSE*'s of the structural coefficients*

| *Exp.* | *No.* | $b_{12}$ | $c_{11}$ | $c_{12}$ | $b_{21}$ | $c_{23}$ | $c_{24}$ |
|---|---|---|---|---|---|---|---|
| | $B_1$ | 0.110 | 0.091 | 0.097 | 0.128 | 0.091 | 0.091 |
| | $B_2$ | 0.192 | 0.145 | 0.125 | 0.171 | 0.132 | 0.125 |
| I | $B_3$ | 0.891 | 0.562 | 0.625 | 1.285 | 0.800 | 0.825 |
| | $B_4$ | 0.252 | 0.173 | 0.190 | 0.074 | 0.054 | 0.053 |
| | $B_5$ | 0.061 | 0.051 | 0.054 | 3.569 | 2.138 | 2.316 |
| II | $B_6$ | 0.157 | 0.137 | 0.151 | 0.147 | 0.171 | 0.164 |
| | $B_7$ | 0.173 | 0.189 | 0.192 | 0.170 | 0.220 | 0.204 |

b. Comparison of experiments I $B_1$ and II $B_6$ and $B_7$ shows that the introduction of multicollinearity decreases the '*exactness*' of the 2 SLS estimators.
   Even a 'moderate' correlation coefficient of $\pm 0.7$ between the variables $x_1$ and $x_2$, and $x_3$ and $x_4$ gives an obviously larger RMSE.
c. Just as with the two-equation model reduction of the non-diagonal elements involves a reduction in the RMSE of all coefficients of the three-equations model.
   (See the results of experiments III $B_8$, $B_9$ and $B_{10}$ and III $B_{11}$ and $B_{12}$). Changing the signs of the coefficients has only a slight influence on the RMSE.

*Table 4.2.11* RMSE*'s of the structural coefficients*

| *Exp.* | *No.* | $b_{12}$ | $b_{13}$ | $c_{11}$ | $c_{12}$ | $b_{21}$ | $b_{23}$ | $c_{23}$ | $c_{24}$ | $b_{31}$ | $b_{32}$ | $c_{35}$ | $c_{36}$ |
|---|---|---|---|---|---|---|---|---|---|---|---|---|---|
| | $B_8$ | 0.165 | | 0.115 | 0.118 | | 0.145 | 0.121 | 0.124 | 0.173 | | 0.122 | 0.131 |
| | $B_9$ | 0.257 | | 0.143 | 0.154 | | 0.215 | 0.146 | 0.153 | 0.247 | | 0.162 | 0.163 |
| III | $B_{10}$ | 0.831 | | 0.399 | 0.437 | | 0.620 | 0.330 | 0.332 | 0.631 | | 0.373 | 0.375 |
| | $B_{11}$ | 0.289 | 0.252 | 0.166 | 0.157 | 0.234 | 0.251 | 0.168 | 0.192 | 0.279 | 0.236 | 0.186 | 0.178 |
| | $B_{12}$ | 0.316 | 0.326 | 0.232 | 0.230 | 0.287 | 0.356 | 0.221 | 0.200 | 0.320 | 0.321 | 0.215 | 0.228 |
| | $B_{13}$ | 0.445 | 0.326 | 0.228 | 0.247 | 0.343 | 0.449 | 0.212 | 0.242 | 0.509 | 0.314 | 0.272 | 0.256 |

The studies discussed in this section confirm Klein and Nakamura's qualitative analysis [1962], discussed in III.6. The conclusion – that LIML estimators are more sensitive to multicollinearity than 2SLS estimators – is supported by these simulation studies. Therefore 2SLS estimators are preferable to LIML estimators if there is multicollinearity.

A second general conclusion from these studies is that the size of the non-diagonal elements of the $B$-matrix is important to the 'exactness' of the 2SLS estimators.

Large non-diagonal elements strengthen the multicollinearity effect in such a way that the RMSE of the estimated coefficients increases with increasing non-diagonal elements.

This increase in the RMSE is caused mainly by the variance increase, as is the case with multicollinearity.

## IV.3 DESIGN OF THE SIMULATION MODEL

The most important elements of the simulation model will now be discussed point by point.

### a. *The model*

As this study is designed as an initial approach to the small sample properties of the generalised 2SLS estimators as against the 2SLS estimators in the case of multicollinearity, Mosbaek and Wold's two equation-model has been chosen as the basic model. This model is:

$$\begin{pmatrix} 1 & b_{12} \\ b_{21} & 1 \end{pmatrix} \begin{pmatrix} y_{1t} \\ y_{2t} \end{pmatrix} + \begin{pmatrix} c_{11} & c_{12} & 0 & 0 \\ 0 & 0 & c_{23} & c_{24} \end{pmatrix} \begin{bmatrix} x_{1t} \\ x_{2t} \\ x_{3t} \\ x_{4t} \end{bmatrix} = \begin{pmatrix} \varepsilon_{1t} \\ \varepsilon_{2t} \end{pmatrix} \qquad t = 1, 2, \ldots, T \tag{4.3.1}$$

in which: $y_1$ and $y_2$ are endogenous variables

$x_1$ to $x_4$ are exogenous variables and

$\varepsilon_1$ and $\varepsilon_2$ are error-terms.

Both equations of this model are over-identified, which is the most common situation in econometrics.

For this experiment, preference is given to a small model for various reasons:

1. It is economically interpretable in such a way that a reasonable economic theory exists on which this model could be based.
   This does not imply, however, that the values chosen in this study for the parameters and the endogenous – and exogenous – variables correspond with the reality described with this theory.
2. The volume of arithmetic will be limited, while the results are easy to scan owing to the small number of parameters. Lastly, this model was also used by Summers, Seibt and Wold and Mosbaek in their studies which we discussed in the preceding paragraph. Comparison with these studies will therefore be possible.

b. *Sample size*

The sample size for the experiment was taken as 20 for the following reasons.

With annual figures, twenty years will be the maximum time during which the structure on which these figures are based can be presumed to remain unchanged.

With quarterly figures, considerably bigger samples might be justifiable.

In this case, however, autocorrelation of error-terms (see III.2 hyp. 2) can no longer be disregarded, and hence the estimation methods now discussed cannot be used.

c. *Exogenous variables*

In this study, the data set of the exogenous variables was not fixed for all replications but was sampled for each replication from a multinormal distribution with zero expectation and a covariance matrix:

$$D = \begin{bmatrix} 1 & 0.9 & 0 & 0 \\ 0.9 & 1 & 0 & 0 \\ 0 & 0 & 1 & 0 \\ 0 & 0 & 0 & 1 \end{bmatrix} \qquad (4.3.2)$$

in which the 20 draws for each sample are independent. This repeated re-determination of the data set of the exogenous variables is preferable since – in examining the simulation studies discussed in the preceding section – there is no denying that many estimation methods are sensitive to even minor changes in the data sets of the exogenous variables.

d. *Error-terms*

In this study, the error-terms of the reduced form are drawn for each replication from a binormal distribution with zero expectation and a covariance matrix:

$$\Omega = \begin{pmatrix} 0.2 & 0 \\ 0 & 0.2 \end{pmatrix} \tag{4.3.3}$$

in which the 20 draws for each sample are independent.

The distribution of the error-terms can be claimed to be normal in that with a correct specification of the model the error-terms will be built up from a large number of factors each having a negligible influence on the equation.

Based on the central limit theorem, the normal distribution of the errors can then be justified.

If only a relatively small part of these factors is present in the error-terms of both equations, then the error-terms can be regarded as independent, and this is presumed to be the case.

e. *Coefficients of endogenous and exogenous variables*

For simplicity, the coefficients of the exogenous variables are assumed to be equal, but they differ in sign so that $b_{12} = b$ and $b_{21} = -b$.

For the same reason, the coefficients of the exogenous variables are assumed to be equal two by two, so that $c_{11} = c_{12} = c_1$ and $c_{23} = c_{24} = c_2$. Moreover, they have been chosen in such a way that the variances of the endogenous variables equal unity. This normalisation has been effected because it extends the comparability of the models, so that the influence of the size of the $b$-coefficient on the estimators can be studied more easily.

f. *Variations of the model*

The simulation studies discussed in IV. 2 show that the most important factor influencing the exactness of the estimators is the size of the non-diagonal elements of the $B$-matrix.

The degree of multicollinearity in the second step of the 2SLS method increases if these non-diagonal elements increase in value. For the present model this can be shown fairly simply. The reduced form of the model is:

$$\begin{pmatrix} y_{1t} \\ y_{2t} \end{pmatrix} = \frac{1}{1+b^2} \begin{pmatrix} -c_1 & -c_1 & -bc_2 & -bc_2 \\ bc_1 & bc_1 & -c_2 & -c_2 \end{pmatrix} \begin{bmatrix} x_{1t} \\ x_{2t} \\ x_{3t} \\ x_{4t} \end{bmatrix} + \begin{pmatrix} \eta_{1t} \\ \eta_{2t} \end{pmatrix} \tag{4.3.4}$$

from which coefficients $c_1$ and $c_2$ can be calculated, with the requirement that $V(y_1) = V(y_2) = 1$. These equal:

$$\begin{cases} c_1 = \dfrac{2}{\sqrt{19}} \sqrt{1+b^2} \\ c_2 = \dfrac{2}{\sqrt{10}} \sqrt{1+b^2} \end{cases} \tag{4.3.5}$$

The correlation coefficient of $x_1$ and $y_2$ will now be:

$$\rho(x_1 y_2) = \frac{2b}{\sqrt{19}\sqrt{1+b^2}} \tag{4.3.6}$$

As:

$$\rho^2(x_1 y_2) = \frac{4b^2}{19(1+b^2)} \tag{4.3.7}$$

represents a monotonously increasing function of $b^2$ and moreover as:

$$\rho^2(x_1 y_2) \leq \rho^2(x_1 \hat{y}_2) \tag{4.3.8}$$

it follows from the above that the degree of multicollinearity between $\hat{y}_2$ and $x_1$ increases as $|b|$ increases.

The same applies to $\hat{y}_2$ and $x_2$.

The two variations of the model studied in view of the above are:

$b = 0.5$ and $b = 1.0$.

g. *Estimation methods*

For every sample of 20 observations of the endogenous and exogenous variables, the 2SLS and generalised 2SLS estimators of the first equation of the structural form of the model are computed. At the same time, in the first step of these methods, the best linear unbiased and the best linear $P$-unbiased estimators of the second equation of the reduced form of the model are computed.

The first equation of the structural form was chosen intentionally because the variables $x_1$ and $x_2$ appear in this equation, and thus there is multicollinearity in both the first and second steps.

This form of multicollinearity, however, is not exact, and exact multicollinearity is required in order to apply the generalised 2SLS method.

This difficulty has been solved in this study by replacing the $T \times k$ matrix $X$ by its weak $r$-approximant $\bar{X}_r$. This requires some explanation.

Let $I_r$ be an index set consisting of $r$ of the numbers $(1, 2, \ldots, k)$. Let $M_{Tk}(X, I_r)$ be the collection of $T \times k$ matrices with columns in the linear subspace spanned by the columns $x_j$ of $X$ with $j$ element of $I_r$.

The matrix $\bar{X}$ is called an $I_r$-approximant of $X$ if:

1. an index set $I_r$ exists so that $\bar{X}$ is an element of $M_{Tk}(X, I_r)$
2. for every $I_r$ and every $Z$ element of $M_{Tk}(X, I_r)$:

$$\|X - Z\| \geq \|X - \bar{X}\|$$

To compute this $I_r$-approximant would entail determining the optimal $I_r$ from $\binom{k}{r}$ possible combinations, which is a very laborious procedure. We therefore confine our efforts to finding a sequence of nested index sets $\{I_r\}$ with:

$$\{0\} = I_0 \subset I_1 \subset \ldots \subset I_r$$

so that in a certain sense the corresponding $I_r$-approximants have optimal properties.

A sequence $I_0, I_1, \ldots I_r$ is called an optimal sequence of nested index sets of matrix $X$ if, for the sequence $\{I_l\}$ and the corresponding sequence $I_l$-approximants $\bar{X}_l$ $l = 1, 2, \ldots, k$:

1. $I_l \supset I_{l-1}$
2. and for every $I_{l'} \supset I_{l-1}$ and for every $Z$ element of $M_{Tl}(X, I_{l'})$:

$$\|X - Z\| \geq \|X - \bar{X}_l\|$$

The $I_r$-approximant computed with this optimal sequence of nested index sets is called the weak $I_r$-approximant.

For the algorithm used for computing this weak $I_r$-approximant reference is made to van Rooy [1970]. This means, for the model used in this study, that in the first step the matrix $X$ is approximated by its weak $I_3$-approximant and in the second step the matrix $(\hat{Y}_2, X)$ by its weak $I_2$-approximant.

Points (a) to (g) can now be summarized as follows:

1. Take 100 samples of 20 observations of the exogenous variables and the error-terms.
2. Compute the corresponding endogenous variables with the reduced form of the model with $b = 0.5$.
3. Compute estimators for the first equation of the structural form and the second equation of the reduced form by the 2SLS method and the generalised 2SLS method.
4. Repeat (1) to (3) but now for the model with $b = 1.0$.

## IV.4 ANALYSIS

In order to consider the properties of the generalised 2SLS estimators relatively to the 2SLS estimators a measure of the 'accuracy' of the estimation methods must be available.

The simulation studies discussed in IV.2 used the MSE as a measure of accuracy. This has the advantage that it is a simple function of the variance and bias of the frequency distribution.

Basmann [1961], however, showed that the distribution functions of the estimators need not have finite second moments, and in that event the MSE is worthless as a measure of accuracy. A second disadvantage of the MSE is that it is impossible to test the difference between the two estimation methods unless the bias is zero and distribution of the estimators is normal.

In that case, Pitman's test [1939] can be used for pairwise comparison of the variances of two correlated normally distributed variables. But this test does not apply, because of the bias of the estimators and the deviation of their distributions from normality, as is shown by figures 4.4.3 to 4.4.6 included in this study to illustrate this.

In view of this, and of Basmann's results [1961], a different measure of accuracy is preferable, viz. the mean absolute error[1] (MAE).

This has the advantage that it still applies even if the estimators lack finite variances.

In addition, a distribution-free test developed by Summers [1965] is based indirectly on the equality of the MAE's. This test makes it possible

1. The MAE equals

$$\frac{\sum_{i=1}^{n} |t_i - \theta|}{n}$$

in which: $\theta$ is the parameter to be estimated
$t_i$ is the estimator of $\theta$ from the $i^{th}$ sample.

to check the significance of the differences between the two estimation methods.

The results of the test are compiled in tables 4.4.7 and 4.4.8, and their study is based on the following considerations. First, a distinction must be made between the estimators of the structural form coefficients and those of the reduced form coefficients.

The conclusions concerning the estimators of the reduced form coefficients can be simply applied to any one-equation model, which is not the case with the estimators of the structural form coefficients. Second, a distinction must be made between estimators of structural form coefficients from the simulation models with $b = 0.5$ and with $b = 1.0$.

Mosbaek and Wold's study [1970] has shown that with a large $b$, multicollinearity is likely in the matrix $(\hat{Y}_2, X)$. This multicollinearity is disregarded in applying the generalised 2SLS methods and one may thus speak of a specification error with regard to the rank of the matrix $(\hat{Y}_2, X)$ for the model with $b = 1.0$.

The foregoing leads to the following conclusions.

1. For the reduced form of the model with $b = 0.5$ and $b = 1.0$: the best linear $P$-unbiased estimators of the coefficients of $x_1$ and $x_2$ are demonstrably better than the best linear unbiased estimators of these coefficients.
   As expected, the difference in quality between the two estimation methods for the coefficients of $x_3$ and $x_4$ was not significant.
2. For the structural form of the model with $b = 0.5$: the best linear $P$-unbiased estimators of the coefficients of $x_1$ and $x_2$ are demonstrably better than the 2SLS estimators of these coefficients. The difference in quality between the two estimation methods for the coefficient $y_2$ is not significant.
3. For the structural form of the model with $b = 1.0$: the difference in quality between both estimation methods for the coefficients of $y_2$ and $x_1$ is not significant.
   The 2SLS estimator of the coefficient of $x_2$ is demonstrably better than the generalised 2SLS estimator of this coefficient. The generalised 2SLS estimators are apparently sensitive to specification errors concerning the rank of the matrix $(\hat{Y}_2, X_1)$.

These results warrant moderate optimism about the possibilities of the generalised 2SLS method.

A final decision can only be obtained, however, with an extensive simulation study establishing the degree and location of multicollinearity for each sample with the tests in I.4.

For the time being, and in the absence of specification errors concerning the ranks of the various matrices, the best linear $P$-unbiased estimators are preferable to the best linear unbiased estimators, and the generalised 2SLS estimators to the 2SLS estimators.

*Table 4.4.1 The mean bias, variance and* MSE *of the different coefficients for the model with* $b = 0.5$

| True value | | $b_{12}$ 0.5000 | $c_{11}$ 0.5129 | $c_{12}$ 0.5129 | |
|---|---|---|---|---|---|
| | BIAS | 0.0052 | 0.0060 | 0.0105 | |
| G2SLS | VAR | 0.0054 | 0.0063 | 0.0059 | |
| | MSE | 0.0054 | 0.0064 | 0.0060 | |
| | BIAS | 0.0075 | 0.0077 | 0.0085 | |
| 2SLS | VAR | 0.0055 | 0.0178 | 0.0171 | |
| | MSE | 0.0056 | 0.0178 | 0.0171 | |
| True value | | $\pi_{21}$ 0.2052 | $\pi_{22}$ 0.2052 | $\pi_{23}$ 0.5657 | $\pi_{24}$ 0.5657 |
| | BIAS | 0.0001 | 0.0049 | 0.0163 | 0.0035 |
| G2SLS | VAR | 0.0031 | 0.0035 | 0.0062 | 0.0033 |
| | MSE | 0.0031 | 0.0035 | 0.0065 | 0.0033 |
| | BIAS | 0.0184 | 0.0139 | 0.0100 | 0.0012 |
| 2SLS | VAR | 0.0142 | 0.0151 | 0.0031 | 0.0035 |
| | MSE | 0.0145 | 0.0153 | 0.0032 | 0.0035 |

*Table 4.4.2 The mean bias, variance and* MSE *of the different coefficients for the model with* $b = 1.0$

| True value | | $b_{12}$ 1.0000 | $c_{11}$ 0.7428 | $c_{12}$ 0.7428 | |
|---|---|---|---|---|---|
| | BIAS | 0.1708 | 0.1263 | 0.0238 | |
| G2SLS | VAR | 0.1140 | 0.0798 | 0.0619 | |
| | MSE | 0.1432 | 0.0958 | 0.0624 | |
| | BIAS | 0.0050 | 0.0189 | 0.0079 | |
| 2SLS | VAR | 0.0207 | 0.0290 | 0.2050 | |
| | MSE | 0.0207 | 0.0293 | 0.0251 | |
| True value | | $\pi_{21}$ 0.3714 | $\pi_{22}$ 0.3714 | $\pi_{23}$ 0.3714 | $\pi_{24}$ 0.3714 |
| | BIAS | 0.0078 | 0.0023 | 0.0053 | 0.0003 |
| G2SLS | VAR | 0.0025 | 0.0032 | 0.0024 | 0.0017 |
| | MSE | 0.0026 | 0.0032 | 0.0024 | 0.0017 |
| | BIAS | 0.0043 | 0.0048 | 0.0027 | 0.0035 |
| 2SLS | VAR | 0.0131 | 0.0121 | 0.0025 | 0.0018 |
| | MSE | 0.0131 | 0.0121 | 0.0025 | 0.0018 |

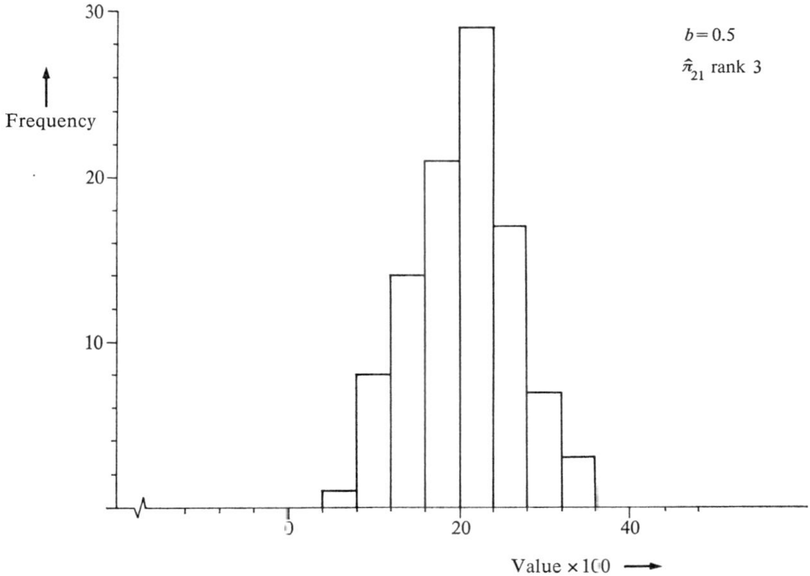


*Figure 4.4.3*

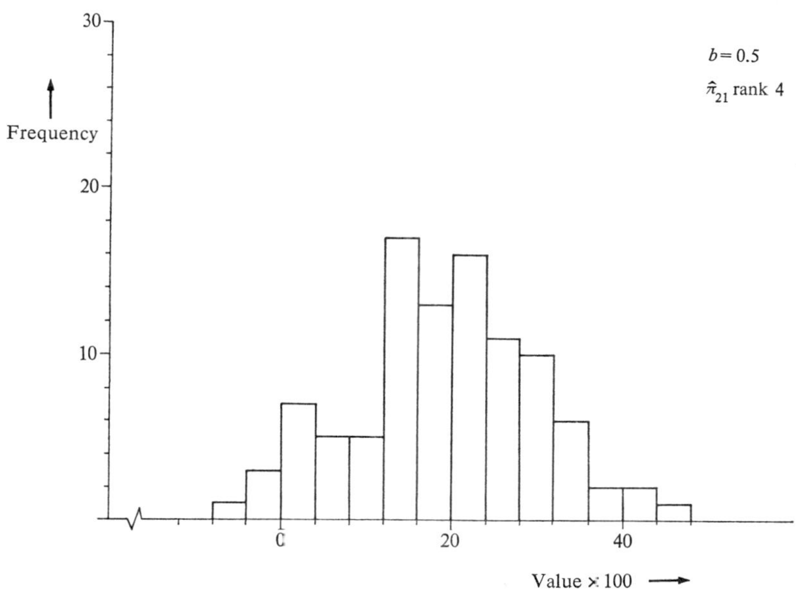


*Figure 4.4.4*

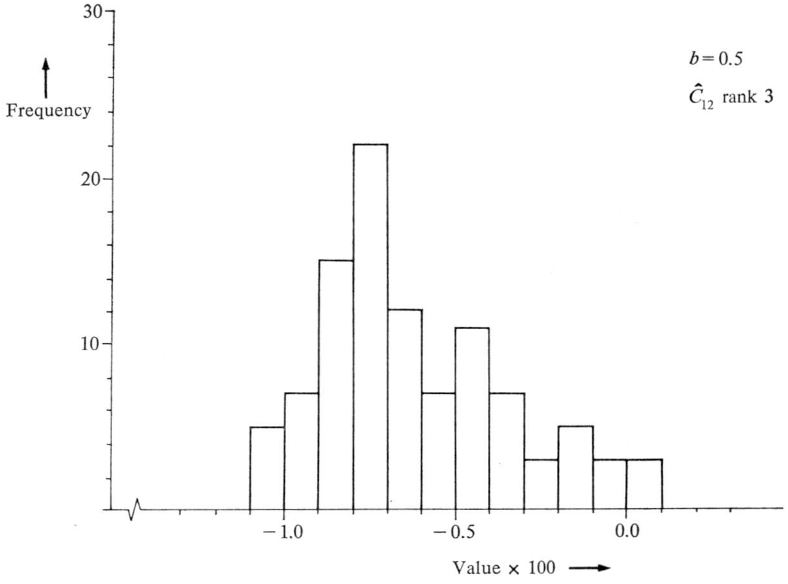


*Figure 4.4.5*

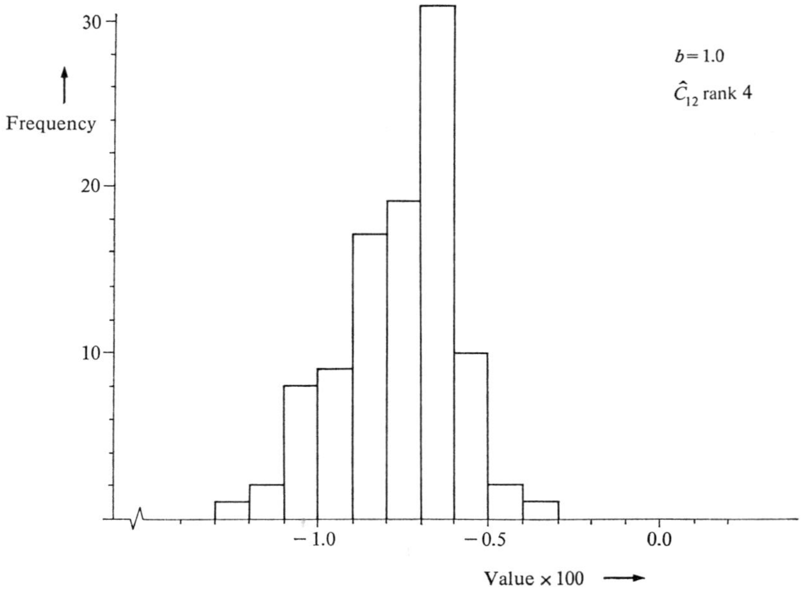


*Figure 4.4.6*

*Table 4.4.7 Summers' teststatistics for various coefficients of the model with* $b = 0.5$

| Coefficient | $b_{12}$ | $c_{11}$ | $c_{12}$ | |
|---|---|---|---|---|
| Value | 0.5000 | 0.5129 | 0.5129 | |
| Teststatistic | 1.2 | 3.6* | 2.0* | |
| Coefficient | $\pi_{21}$ | $\pi_{22}$ | $\pi_{23}$ | $\pi_{24}$ |
| Value | 0.2052 | 0.2052 | 0.2052 | 0.2052 |
| Teststatistic | 2.8* | 2.6* | 1.6 | 1.2 |

The teststatistics marked * are significant at the 2½% level.

*Table 4.4.8 Summers' teststatistics for various coefficients of the model with* $b = 1.0$

| Coefficient | $b_{12}$ | $c_{11}$ | $c_{12}$ | |
|---|---|---|---|---|
| Value | 1.0000 | 0.7428 | 0.7428 | |
| Teststatistic | −1.6 | −1.8 | −3.2* | |
| Coefficient | $\pi_{21}$ | $\pi_{22}$ | $\pi_{23}$ | $\pi_{24}$ |
| Value | 0.3714 | 0.3714 | 0.3714 | 0.3714 |
| Teststatistic | 4.4* | 3.4* | 0.2 | 1.2 |

The teststatistics marked * are significant at the 2½% level.

# Appendix A

This appendix gives a short review of the results of generalised inverses as used in the preceding chapters.

We do not claim any originality in this respect, though the possibility that one or two results are indeed original, is definitely not excluded.

*Definition 1*

A general-generalised inverse of an $m \times n$ matrix $A$ of arbitrary rank is an $n \times m$ matrix $A^-$ for which it is valid that:

$$AA^-A = A \tag{2}$$

*Definition 3*

A Penrose-generalised inverse of an $m \times n$ matrix $A$ of arbitrary rank is an $n \times m$ matrix $A^+$ for which it is valid that:

$$AA^+A = A \tag{4}$$

$$A^+AA^+ = A^+ \tag{5}$$

$$(AA^+)' = AA^+ \tag{6}$$

$$(A^+A)' = A^+A \tag{7}$$

It should be observed here that, in consequence of conditions (4) up to and including (7), matrix $A^+$ is defined uniquely.

The existence of matrices $A^-$ and $A^+$, can be shown with the aid of the following theorem which is given without proof.

*Theorem 8*

If $A$ is an $m \times n$ matrix in which $R(A) = r$ then there will be an $m \times r$ matrix $B$ and an $n \times r$ matrix $C$ so that:

$$B'B = I_r,\ C'C = I_r \text{ and } A = B\Lambda C'$$

in which $\Lambda$ is an $r \times r$ diagonal matrix, with positive elements on the main diagonal.

Matrix $A^+ = C\Lambda^{-\prime} B'$ and is now a Penrose-generalised inverse, since, in view of theorem 8, it follows that:

$$AA^+A = BAC'C\Lambda^{-\prime}B'B\Lambda C' = B\Lambda C' = A \tag{9}$$

$$A^+AA^+ = C\Lambda^{-\prime}B'B\Lambda C'C\Lambda^{-\prime}B' = C\Lambda^{-\prime}B' = A^+ \tag{10}$$

$$(AA^+)' = (B\Lambda C'C\Lambda^{-\prime}B')' = (BB')' = BB' = AA^+ \tag{11}$$

$$(A^+A)' = (C\Lambda^{-\prime}B'B\Lambda C')' = (CC')' = CC' = A^+A \tag{12}$$

It will be shown below that matrix $A^+$ is unique.

*Theorem 13*

Matrix $A^+$ is determined uniquely by conditions (4) up to and including (7).

*Proof*

Let it be assumed that $A_1^+$ and $A_2^+$ satisfy conditions (4) up to and including (7), then:

$$\begin{aligned} A_1^+ &= A_1^+AA_1^+ = A_1^+A_1^{+\prime}A' = A_1^+A_1^{+\prime}A'A_2^{+\prime}A' \\ &= A_1^+A_1^{+\prime}A'AA_2^+ = A_1^+AA_1^+AA_2^+ = A_1^+AA_2^+ \\ &= A_1^+AA_2^+AA_2^+ = A_1^+AA'A_2^{+\prime}A_2^+ = A'A_1^{+\prime}A'A_2^{+\prime}A_2^+ \\ &= A'A_2^{+\prime}A_2^+ = A_2^+AA_2^+ = A_2^+ \end{aligned}$$

This proof originates from Penrose [1955].

*Theorem 14*

The Penrose-generalised inverse $A^+$ has the following properties:

a. $(A^+)^+ = A$
b. $(A^+)' = (A')^+$
c. $A^+A$ and $AA^+$ are 'idempotent' and, therefore, non-negative definite
d. $(A'A)^+A' = A^+$
e. The same space is spanned by the columns of $A^+$ and those of $A'$.

*Proof*

a. This property readily follows, if the formulae (4) up to and including (7) are built up symmetrically.
b. This property can be proved by starting from matrix $A'$ and by showing that, with the exception of $(A')^+$ which satisfies conditions

(4) up to and including (7) by definition, matrix $(A^+)'$ will also satisfy these conditions.
From theorem 13 it readily follows that $(A')^+ = (A^+)'$.
That $(A^+)'$ satisfies (4) up to and including (7), may be shown as follows:

From (4) it follows that

$$A' = A'(A^+)'A' \tag{15}$$

From (5) it follows that

$$(A^+)' = (A^+)'A'(A^+)' \tag{16}$$

and from (6) and (7) it follows that

$$[A'(A^+)']' = A^+A = (A^+A)' = A'(A^+)' \tag{17}$$

and

$$[(A^+)'A']' = AA^+ = (AA^+)' = (A^+)'A' \tag{18}$$

c. From (6) and (7) it follows that matrices $(AA^+)'$ and $(A^+A)'$ are symmetrical, and in view of (4) and (5) that

$$(AA^+)(AA^+) = (AA^+A)A^+ = AA^+ \tag{19}$$

and

$$(A^+A)(A^+A) = (A^+AA^+)A = A^+A \tag{20}$$

q.e.d.

d. In view of theorem 8 this property can be proved as follows:

$$(A'A)^+A' = (C\Lambda B'B\Lambda C')^+C\Lambda B' = (C\Lambda\Lambda C')^+C\Lambda B \tag{21}$$

With the aid of conditions (4) up to and including (7) it is now easy to determine that

$$(C\Lambda\Lambda C')^+ = C\Lambda^{-1}\Lambda^{-1}C' \tag{22}$$

Substitution of (22) and (21) gives:

$$(A'A)^+A' = C\Lambda^{-1}\Lambda^{-1}C'C\Lambda B' = C\Lambda^{-1}B' = A^+ \tag{23}$$

e. This can be proved as follows:
Let it be assumed that $y$ is a vector lying in the subspace spanned by the columns of $A^+$, then there will be an $x_1$ so that $y = A^+x_1$. But then there must also be a vector $x_2$ so that $y = Ax_2$, since, in view of

(5) and (7) the following equation is valid:

$$y = A^+ x_1 = A^+ AA^+ x_1 = A'(A^+)' A^+ x_1 = A' x_2 \tag{24}$$

in which

$$x_2 = (A^+)' A^+ x_1 \tag{25}$$

If it is assumed that $y$ is a vector situated in the subspace spanned by the columns of $A'$, then there will be a vector $x_1$ so that $y = A' x_1$. But then there must also be a vector $x_2$ so that $y = A^+ x_2$, since in view of (4) and (7) the following is true:

$$y = A' x_1 = A'(A^+)' A' x_1 = A^+ AA' x_1 = A^+ x_2 \tag{26}$$

in which

$$x_2 = AA' x_1, \tag{27}$$

so that the assumption has been proved.

The following theorem is often used in chapters II and III.

*Theorem 28*

$$\begin{pmatrix} A \\ B \end{pmatrix}^+ \begin{pmatrix} A \\ B \end{pmatrix} (I_m - A^+ A) = [B(I_m - A^+ A)]^+ [B(I_m - A^+ A)] \tag{29}$$

$$\begin{pmatrix} A \\ B \end{pmatrix}^+ \begin{pmatrix} A \\ B \end{pmatrix} (I_m - B^+ B) = [A(I_m - B^+ B)]^+ [A(I_m - B^+ B)] \tag{30}$$

in which

$A$ is an arbitrary $k \times m$ matrix
$B$ is an arbitrary $n \times m$ matrix

*Proof*

In view of (4) the following is true:

$$\begin{pmatrix} A \\ B \end{pmatrix} \begin{pmatrix} A \\ B \end{pmatrix}^+ \begin{pmatrix} A \\ B \end{pmatrix} = \begin{pmatrix} A \\ B \end{pmatrix} \tag{31}$$

From this it readily follows that

$$A \begin{pmatrix} A \\ B \end{pmatrix}^+ \begin{pmatrix} A \\ B \end{pmatrix} = A \tag{32}$$

and, consequently,

$$A^+ A \begin{pmatrix} A \\ B \end{pmatrix}^+ \begin{pmatrix} A \\ B \end{pmatrix} = A^+ A \tag{33}$$

Pre-multiplication of (33) by $\begin{pmatrix} A \\ B \end{pmatrix}$ yields:

$$\begin{pmatrix} A \\ B \end{pmatrix} A^+ A \begin{pmatrix} A \\ B \end{pmatrix}^+ \begin{pmatrix} A \\ B \end{pmatrix} = \begin{pmatrix} A \\ B \end{pmatrix} A^+ A \tag{34}$$

Subtracting (34) from (31) gives:

$$\begin{pmatrix} A \\ B \end{pmatrix} (I_m - A^+ A) \begin{pmatrix} A \\ B \end{pmatrix}^+ \begin{pmatrix} A \\ B \end{pmatrix} = \begin{pmatrix} A \\ B \end{pmatrix} (I_m - A^+ A) \tag{35}$$

Since matrix $(I_m - A^+ A)$ is idempotent and may, therefore, be replaced by $(I_m - A^+ A)(I_m - A^+ A)$, we find with the aid of the transposition of (35)

$$\begin{pmatrix} A \\ B \end{pmatrix}^+ \begin{pmatrix} A \\ B \end{pmatrix} (I_m - A^+ A) \left[\begin{pmatrix} A \\ B \end{pmatrix} (I_m - A^+ A)\right]' = \left[\begin{pmatrix} A \\ B \end{pmatrix} (I_m - A^+ A)\right]' \tag{36}$$

Post-multiplication of (36) by $\left[\begin{pmatrix} A \\ B \end{pmatrix} (I_m - A^+ A)\right]^{+\prime}$ yields:

$$\begin{aligned} &\begin{pmatrix} A \\ B \end{pmatrix}^+ \left[\begin{pmatrix} A \\ B \end{pmatrix} (I_m - A^+ A)\right] \left[\begin{pmatrix} A \\ B \end{pmatrix} (I_m - A^+ A)\right]' \left[\begin{pmatrix} A \\ B \end{pmatrix} (I_m - A^+ A)\right]^{+\prime} \\ &= \left[\begin{pmatrix} A \\ B \end{pmatrix} (I_m - A^+ A)\right]' \left[\begin{pmatrix} A \\ B \end{pmatrix} (I_m - A^+ A)\right]^{+\prime} \end{aligned} \tag{37}$$

or, in view of (4) and (7):

$$\begin{aligned} \begin{pmatrix} A \\ B \end{pmatrix}^+ \begin{pmatrix} A \\ B \end{pmatrix} (I_m - A^+ A) &= \left[\begin{pmatrix} A \\ B \end{pmatrix} (I_m - A^+ A)\right]^+ \left[\begin{pmatrix} A \\ B \end{pmatrix} (I_m - A^+ A)\right] \\ &= [B(I_m - A^+ A)]^+ [B(I_m - A^+ A)] \end{aligned} \tag{38}$$

As

$$A(I_m - A^+ A) = A - AA^+ A = A - A = 0$$

The assumption has been proved.

(30) can be proved in a way analogous to (29).

*Theorem 39*

$$[A(I_m - BB^+)]^+ = A^+[I_r - (B'A^+)^+(B'A^+)] \quad (40)$$

in which:

$A$ is an arbitrary $k \times m$ matrix with $R(A) = m$

$B$ is an arbitrary $m \times n$ matrix.

*Proof*

That this is true can be proved with the aid of the conditions (4) up to and including (7), theorem 14 and the fact that:

$$A^+ A = (A'A)^{-1}A'A = I_m$$
$$B'A^+[I_k-(B'A^+)^+B'A^+] = B'A^+ - BA^+(B'A^+)^+B'A^+ = 0$$
$$B'[I_m - BB^+] = B' - B'(B^+)'B' = 0$$
$$\begin{aligned}
&A(I_m - BB^+)A^+[I_k - B'A^+)^+(B'A^+)]\,A(I_m - BB^+)\\
&= AA^+[I_k-(B'A^+)^+(B'A^+)]A(I_m - BB^+) + \\
&\quad -ABB^+A^+[I_k-(B'A^+)^+(B'A^+)]A(I_m - BB^+)\\
&= A(I_m - BB^+) - AA^+(B'A^+)^+B'A^+A(I_m - BB^+) + \\
&\quad -A(B^+)'(B'A^+)[I_k-(B'A^+)^+(B'A^+)]A(I_m - BB^+)\\
&= A(I_m - BB^+) - AA^+(B'A^+)^+B'(I_m-(B^+)'B')\\
&= A(I_m - BB^+)
\end{aligned}$$

This proves condition (4).

$$\begin{aligned}
&A^+[I_k-(B'A^+)^+(B'A^+)]\,A[I_m - BB^+]A^+[I_k-(B'A^+)^+(B'A^+)]\\
&= A^+A(I_m - BB^+)A^+[I_k-(B'A^+)^+(B'A^+)] + \\
&\quad -A^+(B'A^+)^+B'A^+A[I_m - BB^+]A^+[I_k-(B'A^+)^+(B'A^+)]\\
&= A^+[I_k-(B'A^+)^+(B'A^+)] - BB^+A^+[I_k-(B'A^+)^+(B'A^+)] + \\
&\quad -A^+(B'A^+)^+B'(I_m-(B^+)'B')A^+[I_k-(B'A^-)^+(B'A^+)]\\
&= A^+[I_k-(B'A^+)^+(B'A^+)] - (B^+)'(B'A^+)[I_k-(B'A^+)^+(B'A^+)]\\
&= A^+[I_k-(B'A^+)^+(B'A^+)]
\end{aligned}$$

This proves condition (5).

$$\begin{aligned}
&A(I_m - BB^+)A^+[I_k-(B'A^+)^+(B'A^+)]\\
&= AA^+[I_k-(B'A^+)^+(B'A^+)] - ABB^+A^+[I_k-(B'A^+)^+(B'A^+)]\\
&= AA^+ - AA^+(B'A^+)^+(B'A^+) - A(B^+)'B'A^+[I_k-(B'A^+)^+(B'A^+)]\\
&= AA^+ - (A^+)'A'(B'A^+)'(B'A^+)^{+\prime} =
\end{aligned}$$

$$= AA^+ - (A^+)' A' (A^+)' B(B' A^+)^{+'}$$
$$= AA^+ - (A^+)' B(B' A^+)^{+'} = AA^+ - (B' A^+)' (B' A^+)^{+'}$$
$$= AA^+ - (B' A^+)^+ (B' A^+)$$

As this matrix is symmetrical, condition (6) has been proved.

$$A^+[I_k - (B' A^+)^+ (B' A^+)] A (I_m - BB^+)$$
$$= A^+ A [I_m - BB^+] - A^+ (B' A^+)^+ B' A^+ A (I_m - BB^+)$$
$$= (I_m - BB^+) - A^+ (B' A^+)^+ B' [I_m - (B^+)' B']$$
$$= (I_m - BB^+)$$

As this matrix is symmetrical, condition (7) has been proved.

*Theorem 41*

A general solution of the consistent system

$$Ax = b \qquad (42)$$

(which means that there is a vector $y$ so that $Ay = b$)
in which

$A$ is an $m \times n$ matrix with $R(A) = r$

is:

$$x = A^+ b + (I_n - A^+ A) z \qquad (43)$$

in which

$z$ is an arbitrary $n$-vector.

*Proof*

$$x = A^+ b \qquad (44)$$

is a particular solution of (42), for substitution of (44) in (42) gives:

$$Ax = AA^+ b = AA^+ Ax = Ax = b \qquad (45)$$

If it can be proved that $(I_n - A^+ A)\, z$ is a general solution of the system

$$Ax = 0 \qquad (46)$$

the problem will have been solved.
Now, the following equation is valid:

$$A(I_n - A^+ A) z = (A - AA^+ A) z = 0 \qquad (47)$$

and it is also true that:

$$R(I_n - A^+A) = tr(I_n - A^+A) = n - tr(A^+A) \qquad (48)$$

since $(I_n - A^+A)$ is idempotent.

In view of theorem 8, we find:

$$\begin{aligned} R(I_n - A^+A) &= n - tr(A^+A) = n - tr\,C\Lambda^{-\prime}B'BAC' \\ &= n - tr\,CC' = n - tr\,C'C = n - r \end{aligned} \qquad (49)$$

so that the assumption has been proved to be valid.

*Theorem 50*

A general solution for the consistent system

$$AX = \mathrm{B} \qquad (51)$$

in which

$A$ is an $m \times n$ matrix with $R(A) = r$
$X$ is an $n \times k$ matrix
$B$ is an $m \times k$ matrix

is

$$X = A^+B + (I_n - A^+A)Z \qquad (52)$$

in which:

$Z$ is an arbitrary $n \times k$ matrix.

*Proof*
This proof is analogous to the one of theorem 41.

# Appendix B

In this appendix we will derive three properties of the Kronecker product of matrices, which were used in Chapter III. For an extensive discussion of this matter we refer to Neudecker [1968].

*Definition 1*

The Kronecker product $A \otimes B$ of matrices $A$ and $B$ gives:

$$A \otimes B = \begin{pmatrix} a_{11} & B \ldots a_{1n} & B \\ \vdots & & \vdots & \\ a_{m1} & B \ldots a_{mn} & B \end{pmatrix} \tag{2}$$

in which:

$A$ is an $m \times n$ matrix
$B$ is a matrix of arbitrary dimensions.

*Theorem 3*

$$(A \otimes B)' = A' \otimes B' \tag{4}$$

$$A \otimes (B+C) = A \otimes B + A \otimes C \tag{5}$$

$$(B+C) \otimes A = B \otimes A + C \otimes A \tag{6}$$

$$(A \otimes B) \otimes C = A \otimes (B \otimes C) \tag{7}$$

*Proof*
Properties (4) up to and incl. (7) directly follow from definition 1.

*Theorem 8*

$$(A \otimes B)(C \otimes D) = (AC) \otimes (BD) \tag{9}$$

in which:

| | |
|---|---|
| $A$ | is an $m \times n$ matrix |
| $C$ | is an $n \times p$ matrix |
| $B$ and $D$ | are matrices of arbitrary dimensions so that |
| $B.D$ | exists. |

*Proof*

$$(A \otimes B)(C \otimes D) = \begin{pmatrix} a_{11} & B \ldots a_{1n} & B \\ \vdots & \vdots & \\ a_{m1} & B \ldots a_{mn} & B \end{pmatrix} \begin{pmatrix} c_{11} & D \ldots c_{1p} & D \\ \vdots & \vdots & \\ c_{n1} & D \ldots c_{np} & D \end{pmatrix}$$

$$= \begin{bmatrix} \Sigma\, a_{1j} c_{j1} & B\ D \ldots \Sigma\, a_{1j} c_{jp} & B\ D \\ \vdots & \vdots & \\ \Sigma\, a_{mj} c_{j1} & B\ D \ldots \Sigma\, a_{mj} c_{jp} & B\ D \end{bmatrix}$$

$$= \begin{pmatrix} \Sigma\, a_{1j} c_{j1} \ldots \Sigma\, a_{1j} c_{jp} \\ \vdots \qquad\qquad \vdots \\ \Sigma\, a_{mj} c_{j1} \ldots \Sigma\, a_{mj} c_{jp} \end{pmatrix} \otimes (B\,D) = (A\,C) \otimes (B\,D)$$

*Theorem 10*

$$(A \otimes B)^{-1} = A^{-1} \otimes B^{-1} \tag{11}$$

provided $A^{-1}$ and $B^{-1}$ exist.

*Proof*
According to theorem 8 it is true that:

$$(A^{-1} \otimes B^{-1})\,(A \otimes B) = I_m \otimes I_n = I_{mn}$$

in which it has been assumed that $A$ is an $m \times m$ matrix and $B$ an $n \times n$ matrix, so that the assumption has been proved.

# Literature


AITKEN, A.C., On least squares and linear combination of observations, *Proceedings of the Royal Society of Edinburgh*, vol. 55, 1935.

AMEMIYA, T., Specification analysis in the estimation of parameters of a simultaneous equation model with autoregressive residuals, *Econometrica* 34, 1966.

BARTEN, A.P. and T. KLOEK, *A generalisation of generalized least-squares*, Report 6508, Econometric Institute, Netherlands School of Economics, 1965.

BARTLETT, M.S., Tests of significance in factor analysis, *British Journal of Psychology*, Statistical Section, 3, 1950.

BASMANN, R.L., A note on the exact finite sample frequency functions of generalized classical linear estimators in two leading overidentified cases, *Journal of the American Statistical Association* 56, 1961.

CHIPMAN, J.S., On least squares with insufficient observations, *Journal of the American Statistical Association* 59, 1964.

COCHRANE, D. and G.H. ORCUTT, Application of least squares regression to relationships containing autocorrelated error terms, *Journal of the American Statistical Association* 44, 1949.

CRAGG, J.G., On the relative small-sample properties of several structural equation estimators, *Econometrica* 35, 1967.

DECELL, H.P. and P.L. ODELL, A note concerning a generalisation of the Gauss-Markoff theorem, *Texas Journal of Science* 27, 1966.

DRÈZE, J.H., *The Bayesian approach to simultaneous equations estimation*, O.N.R. Research memorandum 67, Technological Institute, North Western University, 1962.

DRÈZE, J.H., *Limited information estimation from a Bayesian viewpoint*, Core discussion paper 6816, Core, Louvain, 1968.

DURBIN, J., Estimation of parameters in time series regression models, *Journal of the Royal Statistical Society* 22 (B), 1960a.

DURBIN, J., The fitting of time series models, *Revue de l'Institut International de Statistique* 28, 1960b.

FAIR, R.C., The estimation of simultaneous equation models with lagged endogenous variables and first order serially correlated errors, *Econometrica* 38, 1970.

FARRAR, D.E. and R.R. GLAUBER, Multicollinearity in regression analysis: the problem revisited, *Review of Economics and Statistics* 49, 1967.

FISHER, F.M., Generalisation of the rank and order conditions for identifiability, *Econometrica* 27, 1959.

FISHER, F. M., Identification criteria in non-linear systems, *Econometrica* 29, 1961.
FISHER, F. M., Uncorrelated disturbances and identifiability criteria, *International Economic Review* 4, 1963.

GAUSS, K. F., *Werke* 4, Göttingen, 1809.
GRENANDER, U., On the estimation of regression coefficients in the case of an autocorrelated disturbance, *Annals of Mathematical Statistics*, 1954.

HENDRY, D. F., *The estimation of complete models with errors generated by a vector autoregressive process.* Paper presented to the Econometric Society, Brussels, 1969.

KHATRI, C. G., Some results for the singular normal multivariate regression model, *Sankhyā* 30, 1968.
KLEIN, L., *A textbook of econometrics*, Row Peterson and Company, Evanston, 1953.
KLEIN, L. and M. NAKAMURA, Singularity in the equation systems of econometrics, some aspects of the problem of multicollinearity, *International Economic Review* 3, 1962.
KLOEK, T. and L. B. M. MENNES, Simultaneous equations based on principal components of predetermined variables, *Econometrica* 28, 1960.
KMENTA, J. and R. F. GILBERT, Estimation of seemingly unrelated regressions with autoregressive disturbances, *Journal of the American Statistical Association* 65, 1970.
KOOPMANS, T. C., Identification problems in economic model construction, *Studies in Econometric Methods*, Wiley, New York, 1953.
KOOPMANS, T. C., and W. C. HOOD, The estimation of simultaneous economic relationship, *Studies in Econometric Methods*, Wiley, New York, 1953.
KOOPMANS, T. C. and O. R. REIERSØL, The identification of structural characteristics, *Annals of Mathematical Statistics* 21, 1950.
KOOPMANS, T. C., H. RUBIN and R. B. LEIPNIK, Measuring the equation systems of dynamic economics, *Studies in Econometric Methods*, Wiley, New York, 1953.

LAWLEY, D. N., Test of significance for the latent roots of covariance and correlation matrices, *Biometrika* 43, 1955.
LEWIS, T. O. and P. L. ODELL, A generalisation of the Gauss-Markoff theorem, *Journal of the American Statistical Association* 61, 1966.

MALINVAUD, E., *Statistical methods in econometrics*, North Holland Publishing Company, Amsterdam, 1966.
MARKOFF, A. A., *Wahrscheinlichkeitsrechnung*, Tebner, Leipzig, 1900.
MITRA, S. K. and C. R. RAO, Some results in estimation and tests of linear hypotheses under the Gauss-Markoff model, *Sankhyā* 30, 1968.
MOSBAEK, E. J. and H. O. WOLD, *Interdependent systems*, North Holland Publishing Company, Amsterdam, 1970.

NEELEMAN, D., *Multiple regression and serially correlated errors*, Research Memorandum 15, Tilburg Institute of Economics, Tilburg, 1970a.
NEELEMAN, D., *An alternative derivation of the k-Class estimators*, Research Memorandum 21, Tilburg Institute of Economics, Tilburg, 1970b.
NEUDECKER, H., The Kronecker matrix product and some of its applications in econometrics, *Statistica Neerlandica* 22, 1968.
NEYMAN, J., Remarks on a paper by E.C. Rhodes, *Journal of the Royal Statistical Society* 100, 1937.

NEYMAN, J. and F.N. DAVID, Extension of the Markoff theorem on least squares, *Statistical Research Memoirs* 2, 1938.

ORCUTT, G.H. and D. COCHRANE, A sampling study of the merits of autoregressive and reduced form transformation in regression analysis, *Journal of the American Statistical Association* 44, 1949.

PARKS, R.W., Efficient estimation of a system of regression equations when disturbances are both serially and contemporaneously correlated, *Journal of the American Statistical Association* 62, 1967.

PARZEN, E., An approach to time series analysis, *Annals of Mathematical Statistics* 32, 1961.

PENROSE, R., On best approximate solutions of linear matrix equations, *Proceedings of the Cambridge Philosophical Society*, 52, 1956.

PLASMANS, J., *The general linear seemingly unrelated regression problem*, Research memorandum 18, Tilburg Institute of Economics, Tilburg, 1970.

PRAIS, S.J. and H.S. HOUTHAKKER, *The analysis of family budgets*, Cambridge University Press, Cambridge, 1955.

QUANDT, R.E., On certain small sample properties of $k$-Class estimators, *International Economic Review* 6, 1965.

RAO, C.R., Generalisation of Markoff's theorem and tests of linear hypotheses, *Sankhyā* 7, 1945a.

RAO, C.R., Markoff's theorem with linear restrictions on parameters, *Sankhyā* 7, 1945b.

RAO, C.R., On the linear combination of observations and the general theory of least squares, *Sankhyā* 7, 1946.

RAO, C.R., A note on the generalized inverse of a matrix with applications to problems in mathematical statistics, *Journal of the Royal Statistical Society* 24 (B), 1962.

RAO, C.R., *Linear statistical inference and its applications*, Wiley, New York, 1965.

RAO, C.R., *Generalized inverse for matrix and its applications in mathematical statistics*, Research papers in statistics, Wiley, New York, 1966.

RAO, C.R., Least-squares using an estimated dispersion matrix and its applications to measurement of signals, *Proceedings of the Fifth Berkeley Symposium on Mathematical Statistics and Probability* 1, University of California Press, Los Angeles, 1967.

REIERSØL, O., Identifiability of a linear relation between variables which are subject to error, *Econometrica* 18, 1950.

VAN ROOY, P.L.J., *Pseudorang, approximanten en pseudo-inversen van matrices met onbekende rang*, Afstudeerverslag T.H. Eindhoven, 1970.

ROSENBLATT, M., Some regression problems in time series analysis, *Proceedings of the Third Berkeley Symposium on Mathematical Statistics and Probability* 1, University of California Press, Los Angeles, 1956.

ROTHENBERG, T.J., *Identification in parametric models*, Core discussion paper 6909, Core, Louvain, 1969.

SARGAN, J.D., The maximum likelihood estimation of economic relationships with autoregressive residuals, *Econometrica* 29, 1961.

SARGAN, J.D., Wages and prices in the United Kingdom: a study in econometric methodology, *Proceedings of the 16th symposium of the Colston Research Society*, Butterworths Scientific Publications, London, 1964.

SCHILDERINCK, J.H.F., *Een econometrisch model van de Nederlandse economie*, Ph.D. Thesis, Tilburg, 1970.
SCHÖNFELD, P., *Generalized best linear unbiased estimation*, Core discussion paper 6713, Core, Louvain, 1967.
SEIBT, H., *Schätzung und Prognose bei simultanen Gleichungsmodellen*. Von den Hoeck und Rupprecht, Göttingen, 1968.
SUMMERS, R., A capital intensive approach to the small sample properties of various simultaneous equation estimators, *Econometrica* 33, 1965.

THEIL, H., Estimates and their sampling variance of parameters of certain heteroscedastic distributions, *Revue de l'Institut International de Statistique* 19, 1951.
THEIL, H., *Economic forecasts and policy*, North Holland Publishing Company, Amsterdam, 1961.
THEIL, H. and A.S. GOLDBERGER, On pure and mixed statistical estimation in economics, *International Economic Review* 2, 1961.
THEIL, H., On the use of incomplete prior information in regression analysis, *Journal of the American Statistical Association* 58, 1963.
TOCHER, K.D., *The art of simulation*, English Universities Press, London, 1963.

WALD, A., Note on the identification of economic relations, *Statistical Inference in Dynamic Economic Models*, Wiley, New York, 1950.
WICKENS, M.R., The consistency and efficiency of generalized least squares in simultaneous equation systems with autocorrelated errors, *Econometrica* 37, 1969.
WILKS, S.S., Certain generalizations in the analysis of variance, *Biometrika* 24, 1932.
WINKLER, K., *Multikollinearität – ihre Auswirkungen auf die Schätzung der Strukturparameter in wirtschaftlichen Modellen*, Inaugural Dissertation, Mannheim, 1966.

ZELLNER, A., *Linear regression with inequality constraints on the coefficients: An application of quadratic programming and linear decision rules*. International Center for Management Science, Report 6109, 1961.

(B 1378) Printed in Belgium by Ceuterick s.a.
Brusselse straat 153 B 3000-Louvain
A. Struyf Oude Baan 353 B 3040 Korbeek-Lo